REGIONAL ARCHITECTURE OF THE
WEST OF ENGLAND

THE ROYAL VICTUALLING YARD, STONEHOUSE. DETAIL OF CENTRE BLOCK. 1830.
Sir John Rennie, Architect.

REGIONAL ARCHITECTURE OF THE WEST OF ENGLAND

BY

A.E. RICHARDSON

F.R.I.B.A.

PROFESSOR OF ARCHITECTURE, UNIVERSITY COLLEGE, LONDON

AND

C. LOVETT GILL

F.R.I.B.A.

HALSGROVE

First published in 1924

This facsimile edition first published 2001
Copyright © A.E. Richardson and C. Lovett Gill
Introduction © Simon Houfe 2001

British Library Cataloguing-in-Publication Data
A CIP record for this title is available from the British Library

ISBN 1 84114 127 5

HALSGROVE
PUBLISHING, MEDIA AND DISTRIBUTION

Halsgrove House
Lower Moor Way
Tiverton, Devon EX16 6SS
Tel: 01884 243242
Fax: 01884 243325
email sales@halsgrove.com
website www.halsgrove.com

Printed and bound in Great Britain by Cromwell Press, Trowbridge

AN ARCHITECT'S INSPIRATION

A.E. RICHARDSON AND HIS WEST COUNTRY BOOK

BY SIMON HOUFE

A.E. Richardson in 1930
(AVENUE HOUSE COLLECTION)

EARLY in 1912, the young London architect, Albert Edward Richardson (1880–1964), was ushered into the palatial offices of the Duchy of Cornwall in Buckingham Gate, just opposite Buckingham Palace. He was there to see Sir Walter Peacock, Comptroller of the Duchy and the Prince of Wales' representative. Richardson had been earmarked as a possible candidate to be architect to the Duchy's West of England estates.

On arrival, Richardson remarked on the excellent proportion of the building, designed by Sir James Pennethorne, and went on to examine the door handles. He at once recognised them as having come from the demolished Carlton House, a fact only known to Peacock and a few others! So impressed was Sir Walter by the knowledge and dynamism of the thirty-year-old architect with darting eyes, bushy eyebrows and boundless energy, that he appointed him forthwith on the strength of the door handles![1] It was the start of a lifelong love affair with the West of England.

Richardson came to the Duchy with a well proven and impressive record. He was already an acknowledged leader of a new classical movement in Edwardian London, a school that looked to the past for inspiration rather than imitation.[2] Trained by two church architects, Evelyn Helicar and Leonard Stokes, and one theatre architect, Frank T. Verity, he had already designed two elegant town houses in Mayfair and was just completing the neo-classical but advanced Opera House in Manchester. Richardson described the latter as 'an innovation'.[3] Added to this, he was a well known lecturer, much in demand as a writer of articles and reviews and had only recently published *London Houses 1660–1820*, 1911, which opened up the architectural history of the late Georgian and the Regency, previously undiscovered. It was perhaps the happy result of this research that had so impressed Peacock and metaphorically and literally opened the door to his new appointment!

Richardson was in practice with an architect of exactly his own age, Charles Lovett Gill (1880–1960) at 46 Great Russell Street. Gill was the son of the Revd A. Gill, Vicar of Bursledon near Dawlish, another West Country link. The two men shared their Bloomsbury offices with two older architects, Professor Stanley Adshead and Stanley Ramsay, known in the profession as 'Ramshead & Adamsey' on account of their chaste neo-classicism. They were primarily town planners and had recently rebuilt the Duchy of Cornwall's London estate at Kennington in a civilised Georgian format. When the proposal came from Peacock that they should undertake work in the West of England, they declined the offer but suggested Richardson and Gill.

Within months, Richardson was travelling regularly to Devon and Cornwall, staying at the various Duchy properties and visiting outlying farms. By the August of 1912 he was well at work on a series of cottages for the Duchy, his assistant C. Harold Norton being paid £15. 3s. 3d. for overtime.[4] These were presumably the '2 blocks of cottages on the Plymouth Rd and Lodges' at Princetown mentioned on his Fellowship registration document dated 20 September 1913.[5] These cottages on Dartmoor were to be prototypes for many fine vernacular buildings dotted across the two counties and even into Dorset and Somerset. He was a man who was used to using his eyes and he developed an innate sense of scale and place, grafting these small buildings into the landscape and paying great attention to local materials and traditions. There must be thirty or forty buildings from his hand in the area and its influence was to be substantial in his work, long after he had left the Duchy. Many modern architectural historians recognise the elemental forms and simplicity in these works and consider them to be Richardson's best buildings.

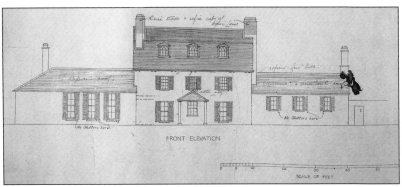

Design for Tor Royal, Dartmoor

But the main task of these years was to be the restoration and refitting of Tor Royal, the principal farm on the Dartmoor estate, as a residence for the Prince of Wales.[6] Whether this was a brainchild of Peacock or Richardson is unclear, but it became a focus of attention and energy. Tor Royal, a handsome Regency building had been built for Sir Thomas Tyrwitt and used by successive farmers. Richardson added a large drawing-room, incorporating yet more doors and locks from Carlton House and gave it a kind of Soane-ish interior. The cornice had a motif of waggons, denoting Tyrwitt's connection with the mining industry. Fine fireplaces were incorporated and his friend, the artist Hanslip Fletcher, was introduced to make pen and ink sketches of the completed work. The house was occupied by the agent and the Prince of Wales reputedly only spent one night in it!

During 1913 and 1914, the partners were making frequent visits to the west, planning more cottages at Bucklawren, alterations to the Duchy Hotel at Princetown and the creation of the largest estate house they were to build, Whiteford Manor Farm. This with its generous proportions, granite storm porch and great chimneys was to have its influence on many later Richardson country houses.[7] Another fascinating project was the erection of a new parish hall at Stoke Climsland. This is a delightful small building, showing Richardson's sureness of touch in a village setting, the whitewashed structure has a welcoming arc of wall and is surmounted by a diminutive lantern. This was to be the original of many other halls of similar dimensions in Gloucestershire, Sussex, Bedfordshire and Northamptonshire. He was designing cottages at Whiteford, Stoke Climsland and Hexworthy as well as a lodge at Chagford and a vicarage for Princetown.

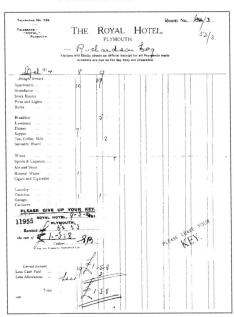

All of this necessitated long stays at Webb's Hotel, Liskeard, the Two Bridges Hotel, Princetown or The Royal Hotel, Plymouth. The price for the latter on 8 and 9 March 1914, including dinner, breakfast and cigars was £1. 3s. 8d. Ten months later, on 8 December 1914, he travelled down on the Great Western Railway in the Penzance Car taking a five-course dinner for the princely sum of 3/6d! The hire of a car from the Two Bridges Hotel was expensive at 18/- a day.[8] All of this travel gave him the freedom to hunt out forgotten corners of the 'delectable Duchy' and visit its libraries and antique shops for historical information. He was a regular customer of Mr Tremayne, the bookseller of 5 Westwell Street, Plymouth, where he procured rare West Country volumes.

Richardson had the use of the Prince of Wales' Ford motor car and was regularly driven from building to building by the Duchy chauffeur Stanier. Stanier's speed in the lanes was alarming and Richardson would growl from the back seat, 'Stanier steady!' His mis-

Richardson's bill for The Royal Hotel, Plymouth, March 1914

chievous side came out during the spy scares of 1914, just before the First World War. Driving through a village on the edge of Dartmoor, Richardson asked for directions in a deliberately guttural accent! Three miles on, his wishes were fulfilled, the next village had a road block manned by a village constable and three boy scouts! The constable flagged down the motor and enquired of Richardson:

'To whom does this car belong?'

'His Royal Highness The Prince of Wales!'

'Drive on!'

The King was said to be amused when this story was repeated to him.

The year 1914 had also seen the publication of his major book, *Monumental Classic Architecture in Great Britain and Ireland During The Eighteenth and Nineteenth Centuries*, a sumptuous volume from Batsfords. This dealt with the neglected civic architecture of the later classical tradition and highlighted a number of important figures in Bath, Bristol, Plymouth and Exeter as well as the more national figures of Sir William Chambers, Sir John Soane, Sir Charles Barry and Professor C.R. Cockerell. This book (like its successor) was dedicated to Prince Edward. This was a landmark work and is arguably Richardson's greatest contribution to architectural history.

His increasing familiarity with the builders of the West began to crystallise into an idea for a further book. For the time being it remained merely a thought, although some formative articles appeared in the *Architect's Journal*. In a forthright piece 'An Architect's Impressions of Cornwall', he distills what he has just seen:

> Yet it is the Classic sentiment of Cornwall which most inspires. One hears it said on every side, that west of Exeter there is a dearth of Classic traditional architecture, but investigation disproves this careless theory, and a journey along the turnpike roads is an education in itself. How one delights in encountering slate-hung toll houses of the eighteenth century, the simple proportions of the humble cottage, and the well-kept farms, the spaciousness of the towns and the prim reticence of the granite town houses. The Classic tradition in Cornwall is not a mild repetition of the matured work at Bath and Bristol; it was inspired by the architectural aspirations of the latter cities, but the local conditions as well as the temperament of the people effected a change in the character. For this reason and no other, the Classic architecture of Cornwall assumes a definite style; it is not amorphous.

Further on he compares the traditional ways, handed down with the kind of work that he sees developing under a new kind of speculation:

> No visitor to Cornwall who delights in a study of buildings and people can fail to carry away a charming picture of the mind, some incident of a market day in Truro or Redruth, some recollection of the diminutive coaches which bring the farmers from outlying districts to the towns, curious vehicles of the diligence type driven by rubicund Jehus who maintain all the racy wit of the West Country. As I pen these impressions of happy experiences, I have before me an indelible picture of snug slated cottages, of sash-windowed farms with vertical slate hanging, generous eaves and massive chimneys. Such a contrast to the brick architecture of the Home Counties is refreshing, and in these days when the evil works of the speculative builder spoil the landscape, it is pleasant to dwell upon a picture of a part of Old England, which, in spite of material progress, retains so much to hold the imagination.[9]

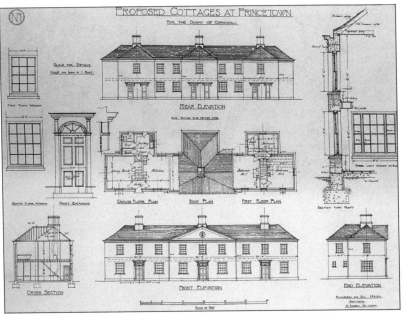

Cottages at Princetown

Although Richardson was to spend the years 1915 to 1918 in the Royal Flying Corps, he was able from his base at Southampton to keep a weather eye on developments at the royal farms. He made bicycling trips into the New Forest and was always about, sketch-book in hand, collecting data for his great work. The year 1919 was an important one for him, not only 'demob' from the military, but his appointment to the Chair of Architecture at the Bartlett School, University College, London and his move to Ampthill in Bedfordshire. Richardson returned to his West Country work with renewed energy, more farms and rural housing were provided for the Duchy and some interesting clients were picked up along the way. Among them were the Amory family of Knightshayes, where he did some work at the mansion and alterations to a dower house. A more extensive connection grew up over the years with the Herbert family of Pixton Park, Dulverton, and with its formidable head, the Hon. Mrs Mary Herbert. He started visiting Pixton in 1922, shortly after the Hon. Aubrey Herbert (part of the ill-fated Tutankhamun expedition) fell ill. After the latter's death, he reorganised a walled garden, planned the planting of trees and created a charming Doric temple. In 1926–7, he created the Town Hall at Dulverton for Mrs Herbert, using an existing building, but reinvigorating it with an unusual and unique iron perron. Thirty years after this, he was to design a chapel for the family, strict Roman Catholics, for the use of the townsfolk. All these small buildings fit naturally into their settings in an unobtrusive way, his training in the Arts & Crafts in the 1890s had not been forgotten.

The most significant plan for the Duchy in the 1920s was the redesigning of the centre of St Mary's, Isles of Scilly, with a neo-classical institute, library and reading room, grouped around paired villa houses, inspired by Regency simplicity.

Although there were frequent visits to Scilly and designs were carried out on street façades and shopfronts, this bold experiment was never completed. A few more cottages were added on the mainland and the earlier ones inspected or extended. Lady Peacock gives a good impression of Richardson's care for detail and interest in the inhabitants of his houses in a later letter:

He had such impeccable taste, that when he went into some of his self-designed houses in the Duchy, he would send some of the housewives scatty, by suddenly, in the middle of tea, standing up and starting to rearrange the room. Of course by the time he'd done it, the room was art with the meagre articles at his command, artistic masterpiece! The next day, if I went back, I would find the furniture vases and pictures, all back in its old place.[10]

The early 1920s saw the research of earlier years coming to fruition and Charles Gill's photography and their joint store of knowledge, made a book on the region a growing possibility. With this in mind, Richardson was anxious to

Drawing of Albert Richardson reading, by Hanslip Fletcher, 1921 (AVENUE HOUSE COLLECTION)

discuss the project with the ageing Thomas Hardy, who lived at Max Gate, Dorchester, very close to where Richardson was building a terrace of cottages for the Duchy. Peacock, who had just arranged for the Prince to visit Hardy, persuaded the rather retiring novelist to see the young professor and give him some help. Hardy had trained as an architect and worked in the West Country building trade, so he was a prime source of local knowledge. The encounter was successful and Hardy persuaded Richardson to include in his book more historical artefacts than just pure architecture, drawing his attention to the iron plaque on the bridge at the bottom of Dorchester's High Street. This was to be included in his next book *The English Inn Past and Present*, 1925. He also told Richardson to investigate the interior of an old cottage at Fordington, then being demolished, as he might find something to interest him. Richardson found an ancient Wessex bacon grill!

Regional Architecture was nearing completion in 1923, the authors using the publisher Ernest Benn, a firm with a good educational and general list but not one that they had used before. It had some predecessors in the Edwardian books that had dealt with the manor houses of Yorkshire or the stone crosses of Northamptonshire, but it broke new ground in its breadth, covering the whole of two counties and its scope, in dealing with the entire range of buildings rather than merely gentry houses or substantial farms. It excluded ecclesiastical structures, even those that might have been said to display regional features, but boldly included prisons, dockyards and town halls which, although showing national trends, still maintained a western flavour.

A new departure was the concentration on small details of stonework and ironwork, which might be said to make up a substantial part of the book. In 1923, not so much attention was paid to fanlights, iron railings, lamp brackets, exterior staircases and sundials as would be today. Richardson gathered up all these disparate elements and made sense of them. On another page he places together a series of stone chimneys from all around the region, showing their richness and variety. A book of this period, even well embellished with good black and white photographs, may give a semblance of uniformity which is not satisfactory to the eye. But in *Regional Architecture* the photographs and text were enlivened by the architect's own thumbnail sketches made on the spot! These give spontaneity and immediacy to the buildings that he is describing, almost as if he was sitting enthusiastically alongside the reader.

When the book appeared, it was not as widely reviewed as one might have expected, but this may be accounted for by the fact that it was ahead of its time. A disparaging review in the *Times Literary Supplement* could see no merit in such a subject adding, 'we wonder that they had the heart to continue.'[11] An architectural press still obsessed with styles was not likely to be interested while the Arts & Crafts Movement had concentrated wholly on the more obvious regionalisms of the Cotswolds and Surrey to the exclusion of all else. The Professor's approach was too subtle for such superficial critics. One of the best reviews was by the author's friend Professor R.M. Butler of Dublin for the *Irish Builder*:

It is as a contribution to the desirable end of forming public opinion, and educating architectural taste, that the chief value of the work lies, rather than its charmingly rendered historic and archaeological story, though this is exceedingly well done. The authors have, as it were, kept constantly before their minds a just balance between the descriptive historic task, and the deductive lessons and their bearing on the recovery of traditional methods of facing new problems.

He goes on:

It is pleasant to turn from the gloomy heights of Dartmoor, with the associations of hard labour and vengeful prison life, to the sunny Isles of Scilly. The authors give an interesting account of the isles and their buildings. They lie 28 miles off Land's End, and are enhanced by the wildness and isolation of the setting; in spring and summer by warmth and sunshine. Many a stormy voyage has Prof. Richardson made to those 'Isles of the West' to superintend the work which for years past he has carried out for the Prince of Wales, not only on the mainland, in the Duchy of Cornwall, but on the Isles which are an appendage of the ancient royal Duchy... For the most part, the building work of the Isles partakes of the character of that of the mainland, but is of a simpler, austerer type. Strong, massive stone alternates with more suave stucco. There is a restrained simplicity about the work that is commendable and suggestive. On the admirable assimilation of the local characteristics, in his recent work on the Isles, and in the Duchy generally, Prof. Richardson is to be warmly congratulated.[12]

A.E. Richardson on Tour, 1930
(AVENUE HOUSE COLLECTION)

It was not known until the recent discovery of a letter that *Regional Architecture* was to be the first of a series of such books. Well after publication, on 18 September 1924, A.E. Richardson and C.L. Gill wrote to Messrs Benn from their office at 41 Russell Square, London W, 'We have an idea that the title of this work may be simplified to cover the other regional districts of England, especially as considerable interest has been aroused by the subject. We are working on four other English districts, North, South, East & Midlands and we should like to work to your interests as well as our own.'[13]

The political climate in the late '20s was not good for these publications and sadly *Regional Architecture In The West Of England* was the only one to be realised. Since that time, however, regional and local studies have gained an honoured place in architectural history. Pevsner has opened up a new perspective on the development of British buildings in general and – in particular – books such as *Devon Building* (edited by Peter Beacham) and articles in the *Transactions of the Devonshire Association* have offered a more specialised approach to aspects of building history. Collectively, they have provided such a wealth of detail that, inevitably for a book first published eighty years ago, *Regional Architecture* has occasionally been seen as outdated. But nothing has yet rivalled 'Richardson and Gill' in its breadth and vision and nothing will ever change its position as the pioneer in the field.

Notes
[1] Letter from Lady Peacock to the author, 31 May 1967.
[2] Nicholas Taylor, 'A Classic Case of Edwardianism,' *Edwardian Architecture*, Ed, by Alastair Service.
[3] Transcript of BBC interview with Richardson 'At Home', January 1957.
[4] Richardson Archives, Ampthill.
[5] R.I.B.A. Archives.
[6] 'Tor Royal,' the *Architect's Journal*, 16 July 1919, p.87.
[7] 'Whiteford Manor Farm,' the *Builder*, 6 August 1915.
[8] Richardson Archives, Ampthill.
[9] 'An Architect's Impressions of Cornwall,' the *Architect's Journal*, 6 October 1915, p.152.
[10] Letter from Lady Peacock to the author, 31 May 1967.
[11] The *Times Literary Supplement*, 2 October 1924, p.607.
[12] Undated review for the *Irish Builder*, Richardson Archives, Ampthill.
[13] Richardson Archives, Ampthill.

TO

HIS ROYAL HIGHNESS

EDWARD, DUKE OF CORNWALL

THIS WORK IS RESPECTFULLY

INSCRIBED BY HIS ROYAL HIGHNESS'S

MOST OBEDIENT AND HUMBLE SERVANTS

THE AUTHORS

PREFACE

THERE is no end to the story of the buildings of England. The writing of the tale alone has occupied the pens of experts for at least a century past, such is the abundance of material, the variety of design and the irresistible appeal of the subject. To eyes unaccustomed to niceties of distinction in buildings of all kinds, traditional work appears the same wherever it is encountered. This to some extent is true regarding the insular character of the buildings, either taken as a whole, or more particularly the general lines and composition of individual works ; but close study of traditional examples outside the metropolis and other large cities reveals the existence of types which are the product of local conditions and for that reason are essentially regional.

A chart of the country showing the main divisions should include : (1) The Northern region which is bounded on the south by a line running from the Humber to the Mersey, and on the north by the Tweed. (2) The Eastern region, embracing the counties to the east of the Great North Road from Doncaster to Barnet, and from this line to the coast. (3) The Midland region, west of the Great North Road, taking the same points mentioned above as extremities and including the counties as far as the Welsh border to a position as far south-west as Bristol. (4) The Southern region, taking in Kent, Surrey, Berkshire, Sussex, Hampshire, Wilts, Somerset, and Dorset. (5) The Western region, namely, Devonshire, Cornwall, and the Isles of Scilly.

At this present attempts are being made throughout the country to re-establish a form of building expression which has the merit of being traditional ; it is essential, therefore, in this study to take into account conditions that formerly pertained, such as local trading interests, available materials, the proximity of large towns, the existence of trunk roads, the navigable rivers and canals and other factors, all of which played a part in determining contemporary prosperity.

Although a strictly analytical survey of the buildings of England would of necessity mean a grouping of five main regions, with Wales treated as a separate entity, and Scotland as a country with its own characteristics of Art, there must also be taken into account the changes in expression that are associated with the demarcation of boundaries both regional and county.

For nearly a hundred years vernacular building expression, which makes up the bulk of national architecture, especially in the country, has been suffering a partial eclipse ; experiments have been made, it is true, by architects to transplant shoots taken direct from old roots, but the ground has not been sufficiently prepared ; the truth being that a vernacular growth if it is to be healthy and vigorous in its flowering needs the care of humble gardeners. Owing to the want of craftsmen, of bricklayers, masons, carpenters and others skilled in their craft, men enamoured of their trade for the work's sake, architecture, the first and the fairest of the Arts, has become a painted beauty, an odalisque to be bought or sold in the slave market at the will of the purse proud.

To re-establish simplicity and good taste two factors are essential ; the first concerns the education of the public, and the second the training of the architect. In addition every effort should be made to encourage builders, and through them the host of mechanics engaged in the realisation of material schemes, to form classes of instruction in all that applies to the construction of new buildings destined to form part of the picture of England.

Architects should be asked to explain their ideas to the men engaged in carrying such theories into being. There might, for example, be Guilds for the different trades in different localities, with architects as Worshipful Masters. Control is necessary and vital to the organisation of building if it is to be raised from a haphazard affair to one of national significance. Granted the existence of a national tradition, which, however, is at present dormant, granted that this tradition possesses marked regional traits, the obvious procedure is for all and sundry to concentrate on revitalising something which exists in a moribund state, attributable to neglect and vicious experiment.

The purpose of this work is to describe the spirit of traditional building as developed in the West of England during the last three centuries. To call attention to the regional character of the style in its infancy, to lay stress upon its development in the eighteenth century, moreover, to carry thought to its later manifestations in the early years of Queen Victoria's reign. Many things have to be accounted for. Primarily, there is the explanation of the development which concerns the channels through which the style reached the people and took on its Doric aspect ; secondly, there are considerations bound up with the influence of local conditions and materials ; thirdly, the historical aspect of the style as recorded in the towns and buildings ; and lastly there remains the benefits likely to accrue by extending the spirit of the traditional manner to modern works expressing contemporary needs of similar intent and purpose. We of to-day are not so far removed from the seventeenth, eighteenth and early nineteenth centuries as is commonly supposed. Times have changed in some particulars, but old customs, manners and habits live long. At the back of this desire for revitalising the spirit of a dormant tradition there is no wish to return to discomfort, there is nothing pedantic or bookish about the theory. Vast strides have been made of recent years by the agency of education to encourage people to look upon home life as a joyous thing. There can be no denial of the progress made in the furnishing of rooms, for almost every person who has the true English spirit longs to enjoy a room of distinction, no matter to what division of society he or she belongs. The people as a whole have determined to make life more real, in so far as the scenic background provided by the living rooms is concerned. The external aspect of convention, be it in town or country, owing to the complexity of modern conditions has fallen short, far short of the ideal. It is, however, a matter of moment to know the public to be ready for good things. The question of reform brings up issues so vast and intricate as to be beyond ordinary control under present conditions. No Act of Parliament, nor subtle statesmanship can hope to bring about the change demanded by students of beauty. Art is above legislation, when pursued by the votary it becomes shy, but the spirit of Art, nevertheless, attends the councils of earnest men and makes its appeal without announcement. The desire for improvement must be real, there is no room for flourishes or ornamentation ; everything that is built, or contemplated to be built, must have a reason to be, there must be a manly desire for perfection tempered with ability to bring about results. The meaning of expression in building must be taught to the people, it must be cried in the market-place, a crusade must be carried on in the Press ; further, the moral advantages and finesse attendant on good taste must be made widely known.

If this were done we should no longer hear the word impossible ; the people themselves would control the aspect of the streets, and would be the first to protect amenities. It is almost inconceivable that a nation as humane as the English should be content to suffer the brutalities of design that masquerade under the name of architecture and should suffer such to flourish amidst the brightest jewels of tradition. Without decrying the pioneer work already done by those who have the welfare of their countrymen at heart it is only just to observe that the battle of reform has not yet been fought. There has been a deal of skirmishing, a vast number of experiments have been made, but few have had eyes to see the possibilities likely to result from the re-establishment of the spirit of national tradition, or at least an observance of its truths through the medium of the people.

41 RUSSELL SQUARE, LONDON, W.C.,
April, 1924.

CONTENTS

LIST OF ILLUSTRATIONS

REGIONAL ARCHITECTURE OF THE WEST OF ENGLAND

CHAPTER I

THE WESTERN REGION

BEING A GENERAL INTRODUCTORY AND DESCRIBING THE DIVERSE FACTORS
WHICH COLLECTIVELY BROUGHT ABOUT THE FASHION OF THE BUILDINGS

THERE are many ways by which the pleasant western lands can be gained. As a preliminary to a study of the humane and material interest of Devon and Cornwall the one from Hyde Park Corner offers the most engaging avenue. Along this road will be encountered links in the chain of history connecting the metropolis with the west country, and to those interested in such things will accrue a lively appreciation of the factors that gave distinction to buildings in places as far distant as the market towns of Devon and Cornwall.

The reason for the definitive aspect of building in this western region is not far to seek. As early as the middle of the sixteenth century Devon and Cornwall, as well as the Isles of Scilly, largely represented the seafaring and adventurous interest of the country ; later on there resulted among all classes a spirit of independence from the affairs of the metropolis, which neither Charles the First nor Oliver Cromwell understood. By reason of this aloofness the west-countryman of the later years of the seventeenth century remained content with the type of house which had satisfied the wants of his Elizabethan predecessor. He may have reasoned : " What can a man desire better than a country house of stone cased internally with oak, or a town house in Plymouth, Dartmouth, Totnes, Exeter, or Truro, with three overhanging stories ? " In the closing years of the sixteenth century taste in the west country desired house fronts enriched with fantastic corbels, spur pieces richly carved, and latticed windows that shimmered like precious gems in the sunlight. There was an instinctive appreciation for the interior decorations of these houses, particularly the wood panelling. The plasterwork exhibited a blend of local symbols with carved representations, often uncouth, Italian in origin, but more often Dutch by transmutation. There were ceilings of plaster, most fairly wrought as contemporary accounts state, to the parlours and best bedrooms, the balusters to the stairways recalled those that carried the handrails athwart the decks of Drake's ships, the fireplaces were of stone, splendid in ressaut and worked stops to show the affiliation of house and church. Oak was the timber for beams and panels, for window monials and jambs. But the west-country people were eager to learn from foreigners. Thus it came about that at the time of King James' accession to the throne there were already many master builders and carpenters in Devonshire who could work a pilaster with a quasi-Ionic volute, and in the seaport towns there were ships' carvers who could work a ceiling beam with at least one, if not two, classic mouldings. At Bradninch Manor House, some eleven miles from Exeter, where one night in 1625 King Charles the First slept, can be seen some

B

fine examples of Renaissance carving, evidence of the early classic invasion, the forms of which are found in the panels and cornices of the Job room, and spreading like mistletoe to decorate the ceilings. A whole treatise could be written on the earliest manifestations of this quasi-classic work, this delightful fusion of the Tudor vernacular with ornaments from foreign parts, as well as from London ; for even in those days London, to Devonshire eyes, appeared foreign, and on that account was accepted as the centre of fashion. No matter the district in which such manor houses are encountered they are peculiar to the west country, and convey the same impression of comfort and appropriateness to their age and setting. Regarded strictly as traditional works they group into a class by themselves, but it is correct to assume that the character of the manor house, of the home of the yeoman and of the humble cottage remained constant from the time of the Armada to the Restoration of Charles the Second. It was hardly to be expected that the artistic influence of the early Stuart Court, powerful as it was in regions near to London, could make its way *en bloc* into the heart of Devonshire, and what little impetus had been given in this direction was stopped when the whole country turned from commerce to arms at the call of the Parliament ; small wonder that taste in architecture throughout England suffered. We have to look to the second half of the seventeenth century for the beginning of the matured style, which formed the regional tradition described in this volume. It is also of interest to know that the tombs and mural tablets to the memory of notabilities placed in the parish churches began to show traces of classic detail and ornament in accord with the dog-Latin inscriptions. To this period of transition belongs the great gateway to the Citadel at Plymouth, which Charles the Second raised, soon after the Restoration, on the heights above Sutton Pool. Tradition assigns this work to Sir Christopher Wren, but there is little authority to confirm the idea. This gateway, the design of which might well answer as a frontispiece to a book illustrating the events of the first decade of the Restoration, bears the date 1670. Charles the Second having superintended the structure in this year evidently congratulated himself on his power to produce a citadel having the lines and strength of Vauban's hornworks. The gateway to the Citadel is chiefly of interest as one of the earliest attempts made in the West of England to introduce an ornate monumental feature as part of a work of military purpose. A far more important architectural event concerns the establishment by King William the Third in 1688, almost immediately after the Revolution, of the Dockyard at Devonport, which for many years was known as the Plymouth Yard. Sir John Vanbrugh apparently lent his aid to the formation of this Yard ; it is certain that he designed the stylish brick house standing within the high enclosing wall above the original yard. For reasons such as those already given it can be assumed that the changes destined to alter traditional building in the western region began to assert themselves very strongly during the last quarter of the seventeenth century. At this juncture the road from London must again be picked up, for the famous highway was one of the chief arteries along which flowed the newer building theories that ultimately reached Devon and Cornwall. Bordering the road out of London between Kensington Palace and Staines there were in the late seventeenth century many new mansions, as well as a fair sprinkling of small houses. Hampton Court was being remodelled, works were in progress for William and Mary at Windsor, new buildings were starting up at Oxford, while Bath and Bristol began to attract public attention, the one as a health resort and the other by reason of its trade with the plantations of America and the West Indies. The traveller by road from London to Exeter in the days of William and Mary gained some slight idea of the vast works in progress near this main trunk road ; he was impressed by the fine houses of the nobility and gentry bordering the Thames, and probably coveted the retreats of the prosperous citizens who could afford rurality. He did not fail to admire the beauty of the sashed windows of the palace rising above Wolsey's turrets at the touch of the magician Wren. Hampton Court at this period no doubt played its part in stimulating west-country patrons and others to have recourse to similar treatments of brick for the works they projected. William the Third brought the Dutch garden to England, and to his credit gave English naval architecture the impetus it needed by the founding of the Plymouth Yard. It is not to be wondered at that Dutch traders found Topsham on the Exe a pleasant port of call, with safe anchorage for their brigs engaged in carrying woollen goods from Devonshire to the Netherlands. There is a closer relationship between the Dutch influence at Hampton Court and the Dutch houses at Topsham than is generally imagined. It is not to be supposed for a moment that the great western road from Hyde Park to Bagshot and from thence to Hartford Bridge, Basingstoke and Andover, fine houses, noble estates and all, notwithstanding the reputation and splendour of the latter, could alone have been instrumental in bringing about the change in the west-country tradition. In the seventeenth century the road from London to Exeter was thronged with carriers and waggons ; the Civil Wars interrupted this traffic at the time Basing House was besieged, but it soon regained its volume. It must not be forgotten that such places as Southampton and Winchester traded direct with Exeter through Salisbury, and that, wherever a great mansion was building, the effect of such on the building desires of the countryside population, as well as on the minds of the people of the neighbouring towns, was in the same ratio to a pebble tossed into a pool, the first splash over, circle inevitably succeeded to circle. From Basingstoke, the dull town, it is an easy journey to Salisbury, where there are extant many square houses belonging to the days of William and Mary, while outside the cathedral city, almost bordering the highway, are the farm-houses that in Queen Anne's day formed the chief centres for the farmers who specialised in flocks of sheep, the latter three thousand strong. Salisbury Plain in those days made ideal grazing land, and in this we see another link in the chain of events which goes far to explain the prosperity at one time of the woolstapling industry in Devonshire and the resultant building activity. Salisbury at the turn of the seventeenth century engaged in two sorts of manufacture, namely, flannels of fine texture and longcloth for the trade with Constantinople, which goods were carried by Bristol ships from Southampton Water in spite of Dutch competition and the Salee pirates. Such a picture of the activities of the citizens of Salisbury must have been seen by Sir Chrisopher Wren in the year 1670, when he made his report on the spire of the Cathedral and ordered its strengthening with iron plates. Beyond Salisbury, near unto the great western road, stands Wilton House with all its attractions of

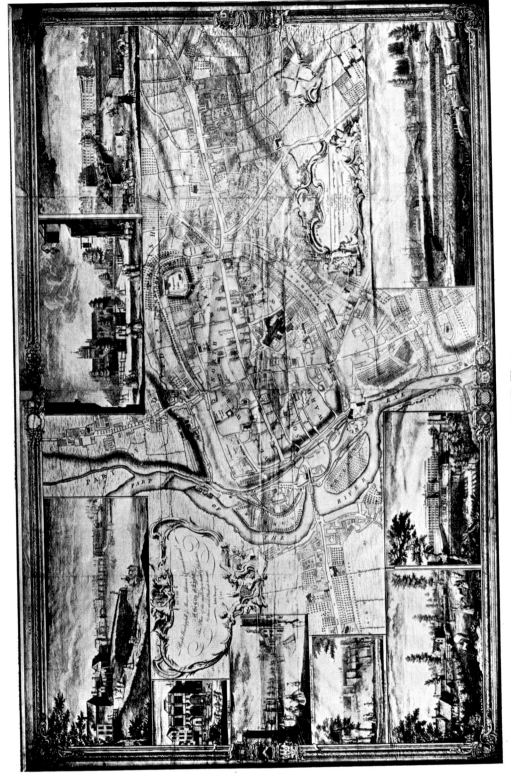

EXETER IN 1744.

From Rocque's Map, in the Guildhall, Exeter.

parks, gardens and fountains, which the skill of Inigo Jones had embellished early in the seventeenth century. And so the western road with its conventions of historic mansions winds on through the fair lands to Shaftesbury, Yeovil, Chard, and Honiton, the lace town, where the buildings of the period under discussion wear an air of state to show their intimacy with the charm of the others already mentioned, neighbouring on the road, and sporting no little pride in their London connections. Honiton at the beginning of the eighteenth century led the county of Devonshire in the making of serge for export abroad. At that time every town of importance in the county was engaged in the manufacture of woollens and enjoyed trade with the Continent. In addition it is interesting to note that from Honiton and the countryside the old Londoners drew many thousands of hogsheads of cider. Finally, the great western road enters Exeter, and there we must leave it for a time.

So far it has been the purpose to connect the main issues of architectural evolution, that developed not quite simultaneously in London and Exeter, by describing the main connecting road between the two cities and also to hint at outside sources from whence distinct traits came. Exeter in the year 1700 was a populous and busy place ; it had, besides the Cathedral and clerical interest, its circle of local society, for many county families owned town houses within its walls. Side by side with Church and society there flourished the prosperous merchant, who owned ships, and the manufacturer of woollens. There was in addition a floating population of foreigners, for the serge market held once a week attracted many buyers from the Continent.

Topsham, three miles from the city, was at this period the seaport of Exeter, the Exe having, by means of the canal formed under the guidance of Dutch engineers, been made navigable to ships of fair burthen ; further works were also in progress whereby ships were eventually enabled to come right up to the lower gates of the city. The major portion of Exeter's trade, two centuries ago, was direct with Holland, there was also considerable intercourse with Lisbon as well as the Spanish and Italian ports. More direct trading with the latter was the function of Bideford.

Any account of the building operations of this period would be incomplete without mention of the chain of small towns in the vicinity of Exeter which owed their prosperity in the days of Queen Anne to the enterprise of local families, who engaged on a large scale in the woollen industry for the Dutch market. Here are a few names of towns wherein the impress of a good architectural style coincided with the success of the local industry—Crediton, Honiton, Ottery St. Mary, Ashburton, of which more later, Tiverton with its noble factory, Cullompton and Bampton. If the red-brick buildings of the period that stand to-day speak aright there could have been but few poor people in these towns, when everybody shared in local successes. Exeter, the loyal city, will be freely described further on in this work ; it is necessary, however, to note that at the beginning of the eighteenth century changes were occurring in its mediæval ways, many of the tall gabled houses that had first graced the streets in company with the building of the town hall were refaced to accord with the spirit of modernity consequent on increased intercourse with the Continent. There are house fronts in Exeter built during the early years of Queen Anne's reign, masking earlier structures, that might well have been

B *

PYNES, NEAR EXETER.
Early eighteenth-century mansion.

imported line for line from Amsterdam; in fact, the broad-beamed ships that entered Topsham on their return voyage brought as ballast many a cargo of rubbed Dutch brick for the embellishment of Exeter. Traces of this material invasion of the city's mediæval privileges are to be seen to this day in the finely moulded string-courses that mark floor stages, also the denticulated cornices that give a finish below panelled parapet walls. It is conceivable that a few Exeter builders and carpenters, presumably through the patronage of the merchants who had made the voyage to Holland, had copies of Vingboon's treatise on architecture, while others remained content with Godfrey Richards' translation of *Palladio* sent down from London by road. At this time, in addition to the erection of new houses of brick, many oak skeleton fronts were costumed with red brick and freshly laced vertically and horizontally with sashed windows.

So far this description of the early work in the western region has had in view the chief centres from whence the taste for the new order of building was to develop on lines parallel to traditional building in other parts of England. It has been the aim to describe the parts played by the metropolis and more particularly to point out that intercourse with Holland helped the development, the bias without doubt for a time being in favour of Dutch ideas. On the other hand, much must be credited to the craftsmen of the period, who contrived to adapt this

EXETER. HOUSE IN ST. PETER'S STREET, 1690.

leaven of foreign design to suit local needs. Not always was it possible to build in brick, there were some occasions when buildings had to be of stone, there were others where questions of cost determined the employment of timber framing for the upper stories, which in turn gave scope for the delightful slate shingling such as gives interest to the period houses of Ashburton and Totnes. It can therefore be assumed that by the time the Duke of Marlborough had finished his campaigns in Flanders, both Devonshire and Cornwall had assimilated the main features of architectural design then current throughout England, the Dutch influence had waned and buildings of good style akin to others of the national mould were rising even in the remoter parts of these counties. In short, those that are extant to-day carry a distinction equal to those deemed first-rate in London at the same period. Although the men who laboured to assert these changes had in view the rivalling of London fashion, they were too close to the picture to observe that local customs as well as climatic conditions were changing the ideals they set-out to emulate, with resultant gain to the development, which speedily became the chief expression of the western region.

DUTCH HOUSE WITH CURVILINEAR GABLE. TOPSHAM, DEVON.
Early eighteenth century.

If Exeter is taken as the chief centre, Bideford and Barnstaple on the north coast of Devon and Totnes on the south are eloquent of the lesser aspects of the newer interest. Totnes in the reign of Queen Anne was more in the nature of a residential country town than a manufacturing centre. Dartmouth, on the other hand, was large and populous, although it could show but few houses of importance. A good trade was maintained in those days between this town and the trading ports of Spain, Portugal and Italy, as well as to the Plantations. Dartmouth thus in a minor way competed with Bristol. In addition there was a considerable trade direct to Newfoundland, the Dartmouth ships returning from Halifax to Spain and Italy with cargoes of fish.

It is of interest to note that when Dutch William set out for England with his six hundred sail of transport ships and fifty men-of-war contrary winds forced him to Torbay, he was at least assured of a welcome from those of his future subjects who knew the Netherlands. Bordering the road from Exeter to Totnes through Starcross, Dawlish and Teignmouth will be seen slight evidences of the early workings of the tradition; still further west but apart from Topsham, it was left to the later years of the eighteenth century to bring into being the matured type of houses that grace the villages and towns on both sides of the river from Exeter to the coast. From Exeter the direct road to Land's End takes the high ground to Okehampton and Tavistock. With the exception of the town hall at Okehampton it carries nothing of notable interest on its borders other than the simple farm-houses, some thatched and others waterproofed in slate. The traveller may chance upon such slight architectural expressions of the later period as classic fanlights and pents, or pedimented entrance doors, but he will search in vain for houses equal in size to those of Exeter and its satellite towns.

The next objective is Plymouth. So far the lower road through Newton Abbot to Totnes and from thence through Ivybridge to Plympton and Plymouth has been mentioned. The fair slopes that border this road show at wide intervals some mansions of early character, for these parts were long esteemed desirable for house building. Plymouth, as previously mentioned, had received at the hands of Charles the Second and William the Third an importance almost equal to other naval seaports. Winstanley had built a fantastic lighthouse upon a rock in the deeps, and Vanbrugh had carried out the fine brick mansion for the Commissioner above the new Yard.

Old Plymouth previous to the founding of the " Yard " had for nearly two centuries been working out its destiny as a mercantile centre. The town had developed from a collection of mean cottages clustering round Sutton Pool, over which the circular fort, built by Henry the Eighth, watched like a stout Yeoman of the Guard, to an assemblage of houses that ranged themselves in the narrow streets face to face, recalling the tall Pintas of Spain, anchored poop to poop. There are numbers of these Elizabethan houses still standing in the narrow streets near unto the Cattewater. If evidence is required of the influence of foreign architectural detail on the west-country tradition that developed during the sixteenth and early seventeenth centuries, it is surely to be found in Plymouth and other coast towns of South Devonshire ; for not only did the builders and artificers imitate foreign ideas of ornament, but even in the humbler sort of houses, where the walls are of cob or of timber faced with plaster, recourse to a finishing colour of pink, green or yellow in emulation of continental practice came naturally to a people who drew their chief sustenance from the sea. It must also be conceded that a people whose interest in shipbuilding formed an everyday subject, cultivated a taste for carved ornament. Here was work for the ship's carver other than the shaping of figure-heads and the embellishment of stern quarters. Such is an outline sketch of Plymouth at the beginning of the eighteenth century when the newer activities connected with the establishment of the naval yard were changing local topography. It is essential, however, to pass on to an account of other places. Plymouth, like Exeter, requires a description to itself, and for this space is given to the salient features of its story in another chapter.

Plymouth Dock, the original name for Devonport, the eighteenth-century appendage to Plymouth, owed its origin to the wars with Louis the Fourteenth. A naval base was required for the fleet nearer Devon and Cornwall than Portsmouth, hence it came about that the naval adviser of King William drew up the scheme for an establishment of the first rank, which included a wet dock, dry docks, slipways, construction yards, plant and all kind of appliances for the construction and repair of ships. By the first quarter of the eighteenth century quite a populous centre had

FREMINGTON, NORTH DEVON. 1820.

HOUSE AT TOPSHAM, DEVON. SHOWING STUCCO ADDITIONS OF 1825.

grown about the naval base. Storehouses of brick and stone had been built, there were ropewalks, laying-by stores, rigging lofts and ordnance depots, together with many houses for the authorities connected with the Yard. Not only did the enterprise of the Admiralty bring numbers of workmen to Plymouth Dock for the building of ships, but there soon developed a town of considerable size outside the walls of the Yard, which a century later responded to the pressure of the Napoleonic wars and was named Devonport.

Leaving for a time the account of the early years of the eighteenth century with its building developments in Devonshire we can enter Cornwall. There are several ways open, first by the ferry to Mount Edgcumbe, secondly by ferry to Saltash, thirdly by the road from Okehampton that takes Tavistock in its length and crosses the Tamar at Gunnislake, fourthly at Horsebridge, and lastly it is essential to complete the survey and to follow the road that runs direct from Tavistock to Launceston. For the purpose of this description the ferry to Saltash is the most important. Saltash was a decaying fishing town when the Devonport Yard was projected, but it had the privilege of sending two members to Parliament, in addition it could boast a Mayor and Aldermen and it exercised powers of jurisdiction on the traffic of the river Tamar. It was the first to receive the benefit of increased trade when the new Yard was opened, for until Plymouth Dock was fully developed the people associated with the new naval base preferred to market at Saltash by water rather than to make the long journey by land to Plymouth. In consequence a slight trace of early eighteenth-century architecture is apparent in the houses on the steeps that lead from the assemblage of sixteenth-century tenements that are now overshadowed by Brunel's bridge. The real development of this interesting town, which is unsurpassed for its natural situation, came in the years following the confirmation by George the Third in 1774 of the original Royal Charter granted by Queen Elizabeth. Near to Torpoint, which is also reached by ferry, stands Antony, the magnificent granite mansion which James Gibbs designed. This mansion, which is pre-eminent among the architectural works of the early eighteenth century, played no small part in changing the sympathies of local artificers in favour of classic design. In Launceston there are to be seen other contemporary examples, the design of which accords with similar works in Exeter.

The next important place in the progress due west is the ancient market town of Liskeard, which at the close of the seventeenth century was reckoned one of the handsomest in the county. There are still in existence some fine examples of early eighteenth-century houses that speak of the days when local society spent some part of the winter within the town. At this date it sent two members to Parliament and was one of the five Stannary towns. It was here that the Dukes of Cornwall in ancient days held Court, and in consequence of the regard in which it was held by the Black Prince, when Prince of Wales, the town enjoyed many privileges. To-day there is no trace of its eighteenth-century town hall with the turret and fine clock, the conduit that formerly stood in the market-place has long since vanished, but Liskeard is still a considerable town, although its local manufactures of boots, shoes, gloves and other goods, besides the spinning looms which helped its former prosperity, have passed into the sphere of things forgotten. In the early eighteenth century the countryside abounded with fine stone mansions, many of which had been built in the days of Elizabeth, some of these expressions of late Tudor times still survive. Callington, the next small market town, has at least one large house of note, the Vicarage, dating from the early years of the eighteenth century and bearing in its lines a touch of intimacy with the spacious character of Antony. This house, built of granite from the neighbouring Kit Hill, possesses a character essentially local. Some years since the central doorway was moved to the side and in consequence the front has lost its distinctive feature. There are, in addition, one or two houses in Fore Street that belong to the same period as the Vicarage. Evidences of the early tradition become scarcer as the western roads lengthen on either side of the Bodmin Moors. We are now in a country which has a vernacular entirely its own, a land of granite, of slate hanging and snug windows, where the cottages and farms hug the hill-sides and take the assay mark, so to speak, of the Stannaries. In the early eighteenth century the newer learning found acceptance in a very slow measure once the Tamar was crossed. The great houses built of granite for the resident gentry in the later sixteenth century exhibit survivals of Gothic

COACHING INN, LISKEARD.
Late seventeenth century.

detail as eloquent in such particulars as the magnificent crop of granite church towers which have defied time. For this reason the number of large mansions of more recent times are few, the old buildings of Elizabeth's day still served for local needs and it was not for another half century that the newer fashion found the rock on which it could flourish. On the other hand, the minor buildings, such as small houses in the market towns, the shop fronts, the turrets to stables, as well as tombs in the churchyards and the tablets within the churches were among the first of the necessary objects to receive a classic stamp. There is a remarkably fine stable entrance of the late seventeenth century at Liskeard, there are one or two specimens of brick-built farm-houses belonging to the reign of George the Second that tell of new theories imported into Cornwall from across the Tamar. The acceptance of classic ideas in mid-Cornwall during the first half of the eighteenth century from the north coast to the south, from Camelford to Looe and Polperro, was cautious ; it is, however, significant that a change was appearing in the outward aspect of small farm-houses and cottages. In the sixteenth century the Cornish farm-house was a diminutive type of dwelling ; as the examples at Tintagel show it was built to a dwarfish scale. The windows were formed of granite mullions and these were glazed with leaded lights. The type persisted until the reign of Queen Anne ; after this the wooden casement window came into being, followed by the sash window, the use of which became general by 1740. The chimney-stacks were built integral with the gables, in bulk they were arranged in two and sometimes three stages, giving the most picturesque effect imaginable to an otherwise severely plain design. Add to this a simple projecting porch, roofs with slates laid in diminishing courses, and doors framed up with vertical pieces, battened at the back and sometimes moulded, and a fair idea of the farm-house or the cottage of the time is presented. The earlier tradition changed almost imperceptibly. Cornish architecture of the minor sort had at this period a style of its own ; there were signs, however, that the masons were not averse to developing something of what was then considered the modern idea. It only remains to study the proportions of the magnificent granite barn at South Coombes Head, near Whiteford, with its arched lower storey and grandiose scale, perhaps one of the finest examples of early eighteenth-century masonry in the provinces, to realise how the principle of sound building was inherent among the Cornish masons, who subconsciously drew their inspiration from the hills that gave them the granite.

Turning to the south coast it will be seen that Fowey shows little evidence of having been affected by the classic tradition in its earliest phases. Lostwithiel at the same period presented a picture of somnolence ; apart from the ancient castle of Restormel and the glorious spire of the parish church, there is little to attest contemporary enterprise. Falmouth, the next town to be considered, is a place that has never lost its prestige, either as a trading town and at later periods as a mail packet and naval station. Falmouth naturally functions as seaport to Truro, hence it was that in the days of Queen Anne the merchants of Truro looked upon the seaport at their gates much as the men of Exeter regarded Topsham. About the period of which this introductory chapter is mainly concerned Falmouth presented many fine houses conceived on broad lines. Charles the Second interested himself in the fortunes of the place when he granted it a royal charter in October, 1661. For years it had enjoyed a flourishing trade, and when it became a packet station for Lisbon and the ports of Portugal and Spain it entered upon a further lease of prosperity which has never since deserted it. In the reign of George the Second there was close intercourse between the merchants of London and Falmouth regarding the Portuguese trade, and a train of carriers' waggons rolled between the seaport and the metropolis in consequence. Truro at this time suffered a little by the prosperity of its seaport and became more important as a residential town, as is shown by a few houses of the earlier tradition that still stand. Even in those days it had a reputation for being well built and honest pretensions to be considered a rendezvous in winter for Cornish families of repute. As the eighteenth century reached its golden age Truro became rich in the character of its town houses, some of which will be described more fully. There are numerous other small towns in these parts, such as Penryn, which in times past relied chiefly upon the results of sea enterprise for their improvement. Another place which came under the influence of classic taste at this time was Helston with its spacious streets, and so by Marazion the western objective of the road from Hyde Park Corner is reached. Penzance, the most westerly town in England, is a place that has suffered many vicissitudes ; it was burnt and pillaged by the Spaniards in 1595, it was sacked by Fairfax in 1646. In the opening years of the eighteenth century, when local trade was exceptionally good, the streets presented a fine appearance. It had a large population, and a good proportion of the local gentry were interested in shipping and, grievous to relate, smuggling. Strange as it may appear, despite the then remote distance from London, some of the larger houses took on an air of classicality, which

Elevation

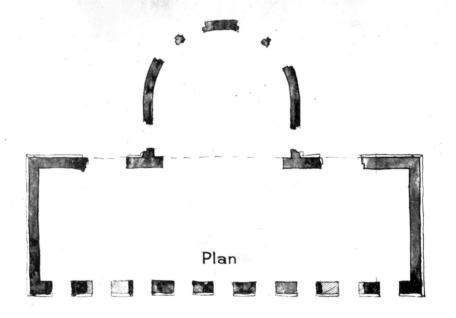

Plan

GRANITE-BUILT BARN. SOUTH COOMBES HEAD, CORNWALL. 1775.

proves the builders to have been well acquainted with contemporary events in Devonshire, Bristol and other parts of England. The style of building for the farm-house and the cottage in Cornwall on the whole remained consistent with that already described as peculiar to local building conditions. It has been previously observed of the buildings of the middle part of Cornwall that slate formed the chief material for roofs. In Penzance, however, a slight change is apparent, for inter-spersed with slate will be found roofs of thatch, both reed and straw, otherwise the materials employed remained consistent with the working of granite for walls and the use of slating in diminished courses for roofs. We have reached the western

TEHIDDY HOUSE, CORNWALL.

limits of the country, there is yet a few lines in connection with the fishing town of St. Ives, where the curious will understand that the early tradition touched a few local features, and a short sentence or so concerning the buildings in the Isles of Scilly—the CASSITERIDES of the Phœnicians and the HESPERIDES of the Greeks. At St. Mary's, on the hill above the town, stands Star Castle, built after the Spanish threat had passed, and modernised in the reign of George the Second. Here can be seen slight traces of early classic in the barracks as in the garrison, but in those days intercourse with the mainland was infrequent, and as the writing on one of the lower windows of Star Castle, evidently the work of a disconsolate grenadier, records, it must have possessed little attractions other than those of natural beauty.

Both Devon and Cornwall in some regard came under the spell of the later

Renaissance at a period subsequent to the counties nearer London.   Devon, as previously pointed out, enjoyed especial advantages, thanks to its trade with Holland ; Cornwall, on the other hand, had the privilege of evolving its own style of design, and in consequence cannot claim to possess either the number or variety of richly designed houses of early eighteenth-century character such as distinguish the sister county.   Both counties in those times, in a great measure, drew their strength from the sea.   We are now to learn how classic taste, once directed into the channels of the western region, was to gain in volume, giving an impetus to building and a peculiar idiosyncrasy to local design destined to ensure the growth and survival of the regional tradition to a period well within living memory.

MARKET HOUSE, CAMELFORD, CORNWALL.   1780.

By the middle of the eighteenth century much had been accomplished to improve taste, not only in London, but in all parts of England.   Mediæval traits, however, still persisted.   We are to be interested in the development of Bath, to observe how the merchants of Bristol emulated the architectural achievements of the neighbouring city, to see a more cultured taste sweeping each year along the western roads to the Devonshire lands and towns and so across the Tamar to Cornwall, until the two counties could boast that they, too, were well to the fore in matters of style.   We are to see the ancient walls of Exeter enriched by fair terraces and crescents ; Plymouth is to develop in a westerly direction ; Stonehouse to rise as a new residential quarter for the families of officers attached to the Royal Navy and to form a stepping place to Cornwall, combining Stoke Damerel with the newly christened Devonport, the latter no longer known as Plymouth Yard.   There are to be many additions to Plymouth and Devonport, for the Admiralty, responding to the needs of the Navy brought about by the later combats with France, embarked upon improvements and additions to the naval establishment, including the building of a vast hospital for disabled seamen.   At the same time considerable developments took place, such as the building of court-houses at Exeter and Bodmin, together with such interesting examples as small municipal buildings like the town hall at

Camelford. Smeaton is to hasten to Plymouth to superintend the new Eddystone and to report on harbour works for Penzance and St. Ives. The eighteenth century had entered on its last phase by the time the matured tradition had flowed along the channels which custom of a previous age had decreed. Latterly the changes were to be inspired from Bath and Bristol, with perhaps a leavening of a few London novelties. The packhorse and the stage waggon still held the main roads, but the stage coach, thanks to the Mail Coach Act, now carried passengers to Exeter within the twenty-four hours, and a corresponding service to Falmouth connected passengers with the packet boats for America. As the eighteenth century touched its zenith many new houses rose like exhalations in Devon and Cornwall. We have the historic mansion at Whiteford, which Sir William Call, a nabob returned from India, built near Stoke Climsland in 1775, with the help of local craftsmen and an

BICTON, DEVON. THE SEAT OF LORD CLINTON.
Late eighteenth century.

Italian or two versed in stucco decorations. This house, although plain externally, possessed some good features, including one of the finest staircases in England. It will be described further on in this book. Whiteford in the days of its grandeur was one of the sights of mid-Cornwall. What remained of the house has recently been remodelled into the Manor Farm belonging to His Royal Highness the Prince of Wales at Stoke Climsland. The influence of such works on local craftsmen at once became apparent in the locality. There is a fitted cupboard in the Half Moon Inn at Stoke Climsland with mouldings corresponding to those belonging to the mansion. At South Coombs Head Farm, a building belonging to the year 1776, the joinery shows a similar regard for refined detail. Close investigation of the towns, villages and hamlets previously mentioned reveals the interesting fact that as the newer information reached the remoter parts of Cornwall it was accepted with avidity by both patron and artificer. There were very few architects practising in Cornwall in those days. Sir William Call, the original owner of the

c

Whiteford estate, took more than ordinary interest in building. It was this gentleman who succeeded in persuading the people of Bodmin to build the Mayoralty building on the outskirts of the town, and it was he, without doubt, who advised on the choice of mahogany furniture for the rooms. The way in which the latest expressions of taste peculiar to Bath and London were transposed as if by a miracle to adorn west-country houses is evident also in the library fitments of Powderham Castle, which James Wyatt superintended, and the splendid design of Glynn, a stone mansion at Doublebois, near Liskeard, built in 1800. By the end of the eighteenth century

ROYAL HOTEL, THEATRE, AND ATHENÆUM, PLYMOUTH. 1812.
John Foulston, Architect.

Devon had lost its hold on the woollen industry, which gradually dwindled in favour of the north country. Cornwall, on the other hand, had developed its mining resources to such an extent that scarcely a hill from Hingston to Redruth remained free from a shapely chimney shaft of brick, many following the lines of a Doric column on a pedestal. It is a little difficult to understand that very few years intervene between the Treaty of Amiens and the time when Trevithick's engines, urged to power by Cornish boilers, raised their beams year in year out on hill-tops and in valleys. The golden age of eighteenth-century life was fast giving place to the silver era brought about by the rule of iron. In this summary of the ramifications of the classic tradition the inevitable juncture is reached where mention must be made of Dartmoor, the tract of desolate moorland sparsely inhabited and rarely crossed.

Thanks to the foresight of Sir Thomas Tyrwhitt, who built a modest house called Tor Royal in 1795 as a dwelling for himself, the possibility of reclaiming certain lands on these altitudes was brought within the bounds of feasibility. A few years later Sir Thomas, in consultation with the Government, was instrumental in obtaining the services of Daniel Alexander to design the War Prison. The labours of Sir Thomas Tyrwhitt eventually resulted in the rise of Princetown, with its church, storehouses and groups of cottages. It was this enterprising Secretary to the Duchy who first mooted the idea of a railway from Plymouth to Princetown as well as the making of good roads across the Moor. Other influences were likewise at work to correspond with the modern movement that possessed England even at the time of her struggle with Napoleon. Here we are brought once again into touch with further improvements designed for the enrichment of Exeter. At this period, 1806, we are to watch the arrival of John Foulston on the rough pavements of Plymouth, with his ideas for turning Plymouth, Stonehouse, and Devonport into a triple sisterhood. Through the succeeding years of the Regency and the reign of George the Fourth taste corresponded once again to the barometers of London and Bath and swung in the direction of Greek. Foulston got his pencil to work and produced some dis-

GLYNN, NEAR DOUBLEBOIS, CORNWALL.
Late eighteenth century.

tinguished buildings as well as new streets at Plymouth ; his methods speedily became the rage, for under his direction not only the crescents at Torquay but the workhouses at Liskeard and Bodmin were built. This pupil of Thomas Hardwick could turn his attention to the design of the Royal Hotel at Devonport, he could produce an austere hotel of small size, such as " Webb's " at Liskeard, or he could undertake a civic centre such as the one at Devonport. Foulston, like Sir John Soane, came wholly under the spell of Greek, which was to the good ; but he had little acquaintance with the principles of Gothic, while his essays in the Egyptian and Hindoo styles are lamentable. Foulston, twenty-five years later, was succeeded by his partner, Wightwick, who changed the style in favour of Italian. One other architect remains to be added to the list of those who gave of their best for the improvement of taste in the west country ; this time it is Sir John Rennie, who combined the profession of engineer with that of a constructional architect. Those who have seen the Victualling Yard at Stonehouse have encountered one of the finest examples of monumental building in England. In the first half of the nineteenth century events proceeded at speed ; the tradition of west-country vernacular building, ever reticent, and ever jealous of its rich Doric simplicity, remained constant to its own well-regulated laws. The astounding thing is that whereas by 1837 it was rare to find domestic work of good style in other parts of England, in Devon and Cornwall it is the exception to find buildings that are not excellent in general outline. Having accepted the principles of square boxes well proportioned with generous eaves and slated roofs, clothed, moreover, with weathercoats of stucco, the local builders, to whom the teachings of Alexander, of Laing, and Foulston passed like rich milk, swallowed these simple rules without question. Foulston in his later days to some extent came under the influence of Soane, and in consequence he was prone to set Greek meanders and scrolled ornament on some parts of his stucco creations, he also favoured a certain grossness of detail in his mouldings, which to a degree reacted on the taste of the journeymen who followed his manner. The fact remains that John Foulston, in spite of the decadence in taste characteristic of the first half of the nineteenth century and the general departure from the canons

THE TOWN HALL, COLUMN, AND LIBRARY, DEVONPORT.
John Foulston, Architect.

of refinement that distinguished the best expressions of the golden age, had, nevertheless, a fine grasp of monumental scale ; he could on occasion impart dignity to the smallest range of terrace houses. Be this as it may, neither Plymouth nor Devonport would possess the respectable buildings they do at this present if Foulston and Wightwick had not fitted them with a stucco uniform such as Nash prepared for the corresponding improvements in London.

In this introduction to the features that distinguish traditional architecture in the west country it has not been possible to do more than touch upon the factors that determined the evolution of the subsequent style. Apart from questions of shape, of the addition of enriched cornices, shapely overdoors, sash windows and richly wrought-iron gates, there is much to be written of the choice of materials that gave the local flavour and piquancy to what otherwise would have remained slightly exotic. The presence of an earlier tradition prepared the way for the grafting of new ideas. In a fuller comprehension of the classic tradition we shall encounter many overlappings, there will be seen few things inconsistent with good taste. We shall find the men of western England conversant at all periods with the handling of material, not only with its suitability as a means of expressing ideas, but with a nice regard for its ultimate effect amidst the natural scenery, and an appreciation of texture values. Once the border between Somerset and Devon is crossed the old buildings wear a look of the country they adorn, there is an air of independence about them, combined with a breadth of handling and a sense of proportion and fitness that is convincing and friendly. Of the local changes much could be said. At Exeter may be seen the ornate slate shingling peculiar to the western region ; there, too, may be seen the unusual treatment of the gabled ends to the brick houses, which had a corresponding development in the Colonial architecture of America. In Devon one may chance upon mellowed brickwork standing in close proximity to cob and stone walling ; there, too, may be seen thatch in juxtaposition to slate and tiles. There is a plenitude of design in door-pent and chimney-stack finish. As the road from London is taken westerly, and yet again westerly, the changes from the char-acteristics of the Midlands become more

HOUSE IN WEST STREET, LISKEARD, SHOWING VERTICAL SLATING. 1803.

marked. Vertical slate-hanging more frequently attracts attention until the houses of Totnes, of Stonehouse and Saltash, as well as those at Tavistock, Devonport and Callington proclaim the old slaters to have been men of genius. The seeing eye will take in all such things which, obvious in themselves, are nevertheless frequently passed without recognition. There will be observed in the front of the London Inn at Redruth a familiar line that breathes of relationship with the houses at Brentford, or chance may direct attention to flutings in George Street, Plymouth, usually associated with the cabinet work of Hepplewhite. The west country has a building tradition entirely its own, just as Scotland and Ireland have their own separate versions of the Renaissance. Because this tradition is simple it is none the less forceful ; observance of its rules will beget acquaintance with the spirit of those who fashioned the masses of material and crystallised as it were the life and customs of the days that have passed beyond recall.

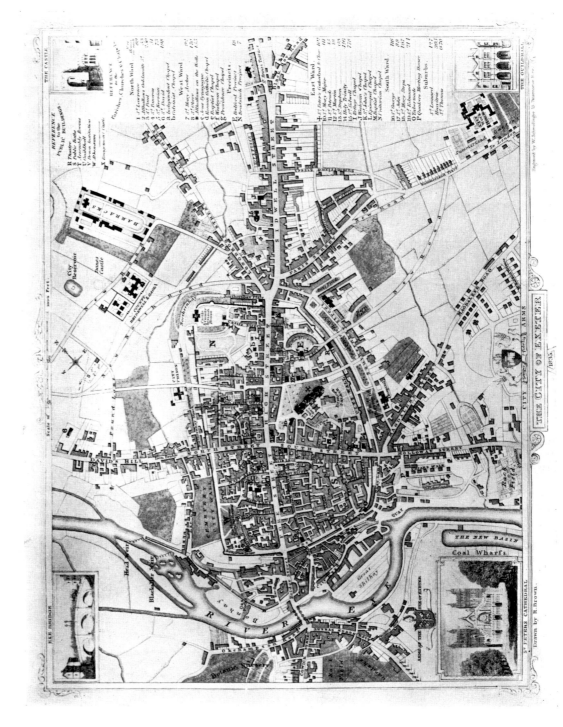

MAP OF THE CITY OF EXETER. 1835.

CHAPTER II

THE CITY OF EXETER

IN WHICH IS GIVEN AN ACCOUNT OF THE CITY, TOGETHER WITH
REFERENCES TO THE PRINCIPAL BUILDINGS OF EACH PHASE OF THE
REGIONAL TRADITION

THE famous capital of the west country reposes on an eminence overlooking the Exe, yet removed from the estuary. Its commanding situation doubtless influenced the forming of the great earthwork at Northernhay in pre-Roman days. That it was a Roman station of importance is vouched for on the authority of Antoninus, who travelled through Britain A.D. 140, and this evidence is corroborated by the unearthing from time to time of Roman relics. Above the tiering of brick and stuccoed walls, dominating the undulating surface

GENERAL VIEW OF EXETER IN THE EARLY NINETEENTH CENTURY.

of tiled and slated roofs, appears the graceful silhouette of the Cathedral, mothering as it were the towers of the diminutive parish churches, and seeming to rebuke the soaring ambitions of the modern spires. From a vantage-point across the Exe the conglomerated buildings acknowledge ecclesiastical authority; yet the secret of their origin, together with the tale of the inhabitants who formerly sheltered within the walls, is as obscure as are the names of the builders. From the tall places and ancient circumvallations can be viewed the windings of the river beyond the limits of Exe Island, and between the chimneys of breweries, flour mills, tanneries,

23

and foundries, trails of escaping steam mark the steel road planned by Brunel. To the north and south rise the feathered tops of hills, and due west the horizon is marked by the outline of Dartmoor.

A good portion of the ancient wall, with ruins of the castle, shows how the expansion of the city was checked, until a century ago it burst its bounds. Exeter is mediæval in expression as well as in the sentiment she inspires. Here ancient boundaries are well defined, the record of her growth is obvious to the curious, but her secret is difficult to the casual.

In outline and mass the shape of the city corresponds roughly to an oblong which is intersected lengthwise and across by four streets: North Street leading to St. David's Hill and Crediton, South Street running parallel to a straight reach of the river and thence by Magdalen Street to the old London Road, Fore Street giving access to Bridge Street and the road to Plymouth, and High Street, the most important, leading through St. Sidwell Street to the highway for Bristol. The Cathedral and the Bishop's Palace occupy a large portion of the quarter to the south of High Street and the east of South Street. Each of the divisions of this approximation to an oblong is intersected by a close network of streets and alleyways defying summary description, although all are clearly set forth in the comprehensive plan prepared by Alexander Jenkins in 1806 and the equally good map drawn by R. Brown in 1835.

THE GUILDHALL, EXETER.

Like most cathedral cities, Exeter still retains a good deal of mediæval splendour; there are the gabled houses in the High Street richly windowed, the somewhat pompous Elizabethan façade of the Guildhall recalling the days of doublet, hose and ruff, the exquisite hall of the Tuckers Company, the ridiculously small, yet exceedingly ornate parish churches, and the great church on the site of the ancient monastery and conventual church of St. Peter, which for dignity of composition and beauty of detail is unsurpassed.

Students of old cities are familiar with the idiosyncrasies of time and fashion; to their discerning eyes a Renaissance veneer of brick or plaster means the existence of a more ancient construction, the bones of which protrude at odd corners, refusing to be denied, for many sturdy relics of the past have been buried

DEVON AND EXETER HOSPITAL. 1741.
General View.

DEVON AND EXETER HOSPITAL. PANELLED INTERIOR. 1741.

alive and a fair proportion of houses belonging to the Tudor period still await investigation.

The Hospital on the map of 1806 is shown (page 22) at the lower extremity of Southernhay much as it had been left by the builders in 1741, the Workhouse was on the Honiton Road, and the old Gaol on the site now occupied by Hayward's nineteenth-century building. The London Inn was standing at the corner of Longbrook Street awaiting its new coat of brick and other additions, the northern side of Bedford Circus (see below) had been in existence for ten years or more, and the

BEDFORD CIRCUS, EXETER. NORTH SIDE. 1790.
General View.

terrace houses forming the northern side of Southernhay were partly built. Barnfield Crescent (page 28) was in course of erection as well as the houses fronting Dix's Field (page 32), both schemes being due to Nosworthy. At this time the stately houses forming the flat segment of Colleton Crescent (page 29) were in occupation. From the above summary and reference to the map of 1806 it will be clear that the first development of the residential portions of the city on a large scale beyond the walls tended towards the south-east on lands enclosed by Paris Street, Magdalen Street, Holloway Street, and the Quay, near the old Customs House. A detailed description of the principal houses will follow.

Bedford Circus belongs to the 1790 period of Exeter's architecture and is representative of the refinement of the day. Houses built in groups have the advantage of producing uniformity and increased scale. The value of a curved line in a group of this description is undeniable, especially when the delicacy of the main cornice is contrasted by the lines of plat bands at two levels following the sympathetic curvature of the brick surface. The doorways are exceedingly well proportioned, and when viewed in perspective seem to check and steady the sweeping range of tiered windows. Not the least of the good qualities exhibited in this excellent grouping is the proportion of the windows and the subtle diminution in height between the storeys. In the year 1780 Bedford House, formerly the monastery of Benedictine monks, was demolished, and the land and a great part of the gardens let on lease to one Robert Stribling, who built the houses above-mentioned.

BEDFORD CIRCUS, EXETER. DETAIL OF PORCH. 1790.

The erection of Barnfield Crescent pertains to the closing years of the eighteenth century, the houses taking their name from a small field in front. From the date of completion until 1830 these houses faced open country, but the development of a new road in 1835 from Southernhay to Summerland Place altered the surroundings. This terrace has the merit of rich simplicity; the front consists of four ranges of windows, the lower being arcuated with double rims. Jalousies, elegant balconettes of wrought iron and a delicately trellised verandah combine to produce a picture of persuasive and refined charm.

The design of the Colleton Crescent group follows in the main that of Barnfield Crescent, and shows the same hand, probably Nosworthy. The buildings were erected about the year 1798–1800, and are to some extent an improvement on those previously named. Coade's patent stone has been used for the enrichment of the entrances, recalling the manner of Thomas Leverton in Bedford Square and Gower Street, London. The accidental grouping of the later houses at the extremity of the Crescent prevents an abrupt termination.

The illustrations include an exceptionally fine verandah, and the delicacy of the wrought-iron balcony will be appreciated.

The range of houses forming the northern side of Southernhay must next be considered, for, with the adjacent gardens and umbrageous trees, they contribute much to the charm of this once fashionable quarter of the city. These terraces were in course of erection between the years 1800 and 1806. They are of lesser consequence than those in either Colleton Crescent or in Barnfield Crescent, and represent a medium form of design between the earlier houses of Bedford Circus and the former. The stepping of the plat band for the intermediate ranges is exceptionally effective.

To the period—1793-1794—belongs the remodelling of the London Inn, with its finely proportioned brick front and splayed wing. The generous scale of the columned porch, with the Greek character of the detail, shows the impending

BARNFIELD CRESCENT. 1798-1800.
General View.

change of taste that followed the teachings of Stuart and Revett nearly fifty years after the publication of their book on Athens. The rebuilding was due to the enterprise of the landlord, Mr. John Sand.

A study of Brown's map of 1835 shows the extent of the city's growth in the intervening period. It will be seen from this particular survey that the development of the late eighteenth-century residential centre, namely, Southernhay, with Bedford Circus and Dix's Field, had been completed, probably by 1810; and further speculations, prompted without doubt by the extraordinary energies of Foulston at Plymouth, had resulted in the erection of a smaller class of residential property beyond the walls adjacent to the four trunk roads. The temporary barracks near Danes Castle had been replaced by others of a permanent nature. The city could boast a reservoir, and the artillery barracks had been transformed to serve as the city workhouse. Meanwhile the outlying streets and cottages were steadily encroaching upon the rural amenities of the immediate suburbs, the bricky tide eventually engulfing some of the country seats.

The Devon and Exeter Hospital, which is illustrated on page 25, was built

COLLETON CRESCENT, EXETER. 1798–1800.

in 1741, the Halford wing being added in 1858. This interesting structure, built almost entirely of brick with stone dressings, stands at the western extremity of Southernhay, facing the ancient Trinity burial-ground. The main façade exhibits a nice variety of composition, the retreats are well managed, and the proportion of the windows is satisfying.

Previously it has been pointed out that the development of the city on eighteenth-century lines was a gradual process, but that, nevertheless, the period, the most prepotent and prolific of all periods with respect to English domestic work, had stamped Exeter as indelibly as it has marked other English towns. Everywhere throughout the country buildings of the so-called Georgian type predominate, both by reason of the intense impressiveness of their characteristics and because of their vast superiority in numbers as compared with houses of earlier date. Indeed, even in Early Victorian days, the eighteenth-century mode was " common form " and consequently excited but little admiration. It was only when the nineteenth century began to exhibit a fashion of its own that, by force of contrast, the reticent charm of the eighteenth-century house was clearly revealed ; and then not so lustrously as it shines out to-day, when the old order giveth place to new so rapidly that " Georgian " relics become correspondingly precious, as, for example, in Westminster, where within the past few years the demolition of eighteenth-century houses has gone on at a scandalous pace. They have been destroyed wholesale with indecent haste. Luckily Exeter changes its mind much more slowly than London,

COLLETON CRESCENT, EXETER.   DETAIL OF FANLIGHT.

and having imbibed eighteenth-century traditions much more gradually, will abandon them with a like reluctance.

For the greater part of the eighteenth century Exeter remained a compact city ; brick houses were erected on old sites within the walls, spacious fruit gardens were built upon, gabled houses in the principal streets were refronted and alterations were made to shops. The suburbs forming the outlying portions of the parishes of St. David's, St. Thomas's, St. Sidwell's, Alphington, St. Leonard's, and Heavitree, for the most part consisted of fields, market gardens and nurseries, with a number of country seats, including Cleave, Exwick, Madford, Ballair, Mount Radford, Alphington House, and Franklin, resembling a ring of isolated forts beyond the inner ramparts. There were a few houses built towards St. David's Hill, cottages and small houses in St. Sidwell Street, Paris Street, Magdalen Street, and Holloway Street and a corresponding development in Alphington Street beyond Exe Bridge. Fresh impetus, however, was given to the city's growth during the last quarter of the century, especially from 1790 onwards, until at the time of the Napoleonic threat high-class building speculation was at its zenith. At this period temporary barracks for infantry and cavalry were arranged on a site near Danes Castle, and artillery barracks were built on the Exmouth road about a mile from the centre of the city.

The London coaches in 1835, notwithstanding revised time-tables, the Quick-silver Mail and improved roads, still took eighteen hours or more to make the journey ; and the city, despite its craving for expansion, wore at this date, if the old prints are to be believed, an air of somnolent nonchalance. A year or two later a distinct

THE LONDON INN, EXETER. 1793-1794.

SOUTHERNHAY, EXETER. TERRACE HOUSES. 1800-1806.

EXETER. HOUSE AT ENTRANCE TO DIX'S FIELD. 1809.
The birthplace of the late Rev. S. Baring-Gould.

DIX'S FIELD. DETAIL OF BALUSTRADE AND WINDOWS.

DEVON AND EXETER INSTITUTE, EXETER.
ENTRANCE DOORWAY.

similar developments at Bristol and Clifton, for the buildings of Exeter have characteristics in common with, and approach in some particulars the best qualities of, buildings of like type in London.

Difficulties of assigning a date sometimes arise from the combination of old and new work. For example, to a Georgian housefront of the first half of the eighteenth century a circular bow window was added at the beginning of the nineteenth century,

WROUGHT-IRON LAMP STANDARD.
DIX'S FIELD, EXETER. 1809.

improvement was effected ; Goldsmith Street was widened, the Higher or Eastern Market was built to complement the Lower or Western Market opened in 1836, and the city was made ready, not to withstand another of the sieges which made up the romance of its history, but to receive the railway. From this summary of the aspect of Exeter as it appeared during a very interesting and peaceful period of its existence the reader is invited to analyse the principal buildings evolved by the skill and genius of local architects.

He will be pleasantly surprised with the variety of type and the novelty of detail ; favourable comparison can be made with

D

DEVON AND EXETER INSTITUTE, EXETER. LIBRARY.

and at a later period the front received a coating of stucco, the resultant effect being pleasant but confusing to the uninitiated.

The famous stone bridge across the river Exe was demolished a few years ago; it had succeeded a mediæval bridge built in 1250. An Act for erecting a new bridge and forming a more convenient approach to the city was passed in 1769 and the foundation-stone was laid on the 4th October, in 1770. A London architect named Dixon was entrusted with the work, but during its progress in 1775 a high flood swept away the insufficient foundations, and the designer was dismissed. This led to the employment of John Goodwin, who had been an assistant to Dixon. A fresh

EXWICK HOUSE, EXETER. 1820.

design was prepared and the foundation-stone of the first arch was laid on the 15th of July, 1776, the bridge being opened for traffic in 1778.

One of the most convincing improvements of the 1808 period is to be found in the terrace groups forming two sides of the rectangle called Dix's Field, the entrance to which is asymmetrical, but pleasingly informal. This improvement was due to the enterprise of the architect-builder Nosworthy. Delicately wrought lamp standards of obelisk form mark the entrance. The corner house, the birthplace of the late Rev. S. Baring-Gould, shows a novel treatment of bow window and crinoline verandah; while the subsidiary groupings, although they have an appearance of undue deportment, are refined to a degree, and relieved from

SOUTHERNHAY HOUSE, EXETER.
Regency Period.

monotony by the treatment of the detail. The balconies are of wrought iron of light scantling, the windows are of good shape and the brickwork is contrasted with stone dressings. Balusters are grouped in panels over the upper windows to increase the vertical effect as well as to act as foils to the fenestration.

Exeter Institute, a distinguished building, stands in the precincts of the Cathedral, facing the wall of the north aisle. The photograph shows (page 33) the details of the entrance doorway and side lights. These details are quite remarkably reminiscent of certain phases of Colonial work. This Institute was designed in the

VIEW OF BRIDGE, SOUTHERNHAY. 1814.

opening years of the last century; it is practically of the same date as the Cottonian Library at Plymouth which Foulston designed, and if not actually from the pencil of this architect it proves his influence. The library is effectively lighted from a circular lantern. There is a gallery dividing the interior into two heights, and the bookshelves and cases form integral features of the treatment.

Exwick House (page 35) is a well-proportioned building, typical of the fashion of 1820 as developed by Foulston in Devon and Cornwall. Simplicity and directness are its chief qualities.

Southernhay House (page 36) is representative of the large type of middle-class town house built a century ago, a novel feature of the setting being the placing of

PENNSYLVANIA CRESCENT, EXETER. 1823.

COLLETON CRESCENT, EXETER. VERANDAH.

the front some distance back from the road, with a small drive and screen of trees. The entrance is masked by a continuous loggia, which forms the chief architectural feature. The slightly projecting centre to the loggia, with breaks and pediment, is somewhat daring in adjustment, but its effectiveness is convincing.

As one walks from Southernhay to the Cathedral along a secluded side path that cuts through the city wall, the small iron bridge arrests attention. It is graceful in line and richly simple. The lower rib of the girder bears the inscription :

"BURNET PATCH ESQ^r MAYOR. 1814.
R. TREWMAN ESQ^r RECEIVER."

Another interesting example of the development of a local residential centre is to be seen in the group of five houses called Pennsylvania Crescent, to the north-east of the city. These houses can be compared with the villas designed by John Foulston at Plymouth, the detail of the verandahs, pilasters and entrances being similar. They are in marked contrast to the modern gabled villas now stretching in the direction of Pinhoe. Rougemont House is chiefly of interest for the admirable grouping of its subsidiary features, namely, the flat segmental bows and the iron verandah over.

About the time Plymouth and Devonport were receiving weather-coats of stucco and slate, many old buildings in Exeter, especially those forming shop premises in High Street and Fore Street, were brought

THE LOWER MARKET, EXETER. 1835–1836.
Charles Fowler, Architect.

into the fashion that followed the doctrines of Soane. The illustration of " The Mint " (page 41) shows the novel treatment accorded to a small shop near the High Street. In the design of this shop-front will be seen evidence of " Empire " character. The end pilasters have Greek key ornamentation, the intermediate posts being moulded. The charm of the design is its simplicity, rendered more effective by the sashing of the shop window.

From the year 1830 onwards Greek detail became the medium favoured by Exeter architects, although local characteristics were by no means ignored. The obelisk near South Street and the doorheads in Fore Street typify the minor features of the day.

In this connection the name of Charles Fowler, a local architect, is of interest, for the erection of two important civic buildings within the city fell to his lot ; but this was subsequent to his success in London. Charles Fowler was born in 1792 and gained experience and training in the office of an Exeter surveyor whose practice included many local houses. In 1814 Fowler made his way to London and was engaged by David Laing as an assistant. He spent some time with Laing preparing

THE LOWER MARKET, EXETER. 1835–1836.
Charles Fowler, Architect.

drawings in connection with the New Customs House, and appears to have started practice for himself soon after. His first work of magnitude was Covent Garden Market, which he completed in 1830. A year later he was commissioned to design Hungerford Market, the scale of which can be judged from his original drawings now in the collection of the Royal Institute of British Architects. In 1835, news of his fame as a specialist in market design having reached Exeter, the authorities invited him to design the Lower or Western Market, which he completed a year later. The illustration on this page shows the fine scale of this building, the refinement of the ornament, the originality of the conception and the correctness of expression,

SHOP FRONT. THE MINT, EXETER.
Regency Period.

THE HIGHER MARKET, QUEEN STREET, EXETER. 1838.
Charles Fowler, Architect.

THE HIGHER MARKET, QUEEN STREET, EXETER. DETAIL OF PEDIMENT. 1838.
Charles Fowler, Architect.

THE HIGHER MARKET, QUEEN STREET, EXETER. DETAIL OF COLUMNS AND GRILLE. 1838.
Charles Fowler, Architect.

THE HIGHER MARKET, QUEEN STREET, EXETER. 1838.
Charles Fowler, Architect.

for it is unmistakably a market and nothing else. That he was proud of his work is obvious from the fact that he caused his name to be chiselled on the stone beam over the central entrance in Fore Street.

Fowler's designs were always consistent, the theme of the conception appearing both externally and internally. He could arrange a classic clerestory, could borrow ideas from the timber construction advocated by Philibert de l'Orme and give substantial interest for the accommodation. Fowler in this essay combined Italian composition with Greek detail, and succeeded in producing a building both

SHOP FRONT IN FORE STREET, EXETER. 1820.

monumental and useful. A year later he was commissioned to erect the Higher Market in Queen Street, a building the exterior appearance of which is characteristically Greek of Empire stamp.

The illustrations show the taste of this designer, and provide an object-lesson in refinement. It has been said of this building that it is as modern in appearance as it was at the time of its erection ; it certainly makes the appeal of its purpose, and is far more logical than many of the hybrid structures produced to meet similar conditions during the last thirty years. In the intervals of his work on market buildings Fowler found time to study the design of bridges. He entered the competition for London Bridge in 1822 and gained the first premium, but John

COLONEL HEBERDEN'S HOUSE, ST. DAVID'S HILL, EXETER.
Early nineteenth century.

ROUGEMONT HOUSE, EXETER. 1820.

Rennie was employed in his place. Four years later Fowler built the bridge over the Dart at Totnes. He had many pupils and followers, and it is possible that the design of the Exeter Dispensary was influenced by him.

Fowler frequently exhibited his work at the Paris Salon, and was a prominent member of the Royal Institute in its early days.

The foregoing account of the prominent buildings of Exeter evolved between the years 1740 and 1840 is by no means exhaustive of the wealth of the tradition, but it will serve the purpose of indexing a peculiar local phrase.

The visitor to the city is confronted by a series of good buildings ; he can read the story of the English Renaissance in all quarters, and he can satisfy his taste for particular phrases, be they mediæval, Georgian or matured classic. Exeter is a pleasant city, busy at the centre, expeditious on the outskirts, allied to the sea and rejoicing in the decoration afforded by the greenery of leafy open spaces. She is mediæval in sentiment, but interesting in the lines of her later expression, which include the warm brick houses of the eighteenth century, the equally warm stucco of a later period, the rugged mass of Hayward's Prison, and the Corinthian insulations of the old Post Office.

Exeter has been taken as a leading subject to show the outstanding features of building in the western region during the eighteenth and nineteenth centuries. In the next chapter Plymouth will be described. The general development of each phase has been dealt with under a comprehensive title as will be seen further on.

CHAPTER III

PLYMOUTH, STONEHOUSE, AND DEVONPORT

BEING AN ACCOUNT OF THE DEVELOPMENT OF THE THREE TOWNS FROM THE TIME OF THE TUDORS TO THE PRESENT DAY

THE real capital of the west country is the ancient maritime seaport of Plymouth, which embraces to-day the naval centre of Devonport and the diminutive township of Stonehouse, the latter wedged between two arms of the sea. Exeter is the official metropolis of Devonshire and Bodmin of Cornwall, but these places are of secondary importance to the three

SUTTON POOL AND CUSTOM HOUSE, PLYMOUTH.
Early nineteenth century.

towns which have developed in the centuries, along the water's edge, and above the heights to form a triple sisterhood. The towns follow the coast line from the confluence of the Plym and the Cattewater, along the foreshore of the Sound, doubling Millbay and continuing up the Hamoaze, forming a gigantic bow of eight miles, to which the serrations of the coast are subordinate. No situation could be better devised for a great naval centre ; yet Plymouth with its historical associations is the product of centuries of slow growth, it is allied to the sea from which it draws its sustenance, and it is sheltered naturally and artificially from attack. From the famous Hoe at sunset the flash of the Eddystone can be caught, away to the west the Cornish hills dissolve into a golden haze, and to the north, above the cool green

47

uplands, rise the grim heights of Dartmoor swathed in drifting clouds of mist. Westward in the middle distance the reaches of the Hamoaze and other landlocked waters mark the estuary of the Tamar, where fighting leviathans ride at anchor, and southward is the Sound, jewelled with Drake's Island and bounded by the peninsula of the Cornish shore, the great breakwater and an arm of Devon. Plymouth, notwithstanding its natural advantages, pays toll for its position when westerly gales sweep up Channel ; it wears a waterproof mantle of slate and stucco, in foul weather and fine, for the wind-driven rain and damp sea fogs assail the crevices when gales blow unchecked. To understand Plymouth one must live there, no

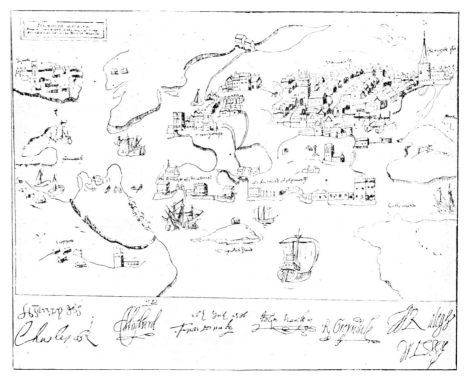

MAP OF PLYMOUTH (Early sixteenth century).
British Museum Collection.

cursory inspection will suffice to wrest the secret of the place from the maze of intricacies which make up this extraordinary assemblage of houses, peopled by over 250,000 inhabitants. Other cities in the kingdom differ by reason of the sentiment they inspire, they all have devotees, but mother Plymouth is a guardian of the sea, to her it is life, and from such associations her whimsicalities have emerged. She is still Elizabethan and adventurous, despite the motley of the newer suburbs and the decay of the old town menaced as it is by a ring of breweries and gasworks. Many actors of the past—kings, queens, ambassadors, admirals and soldiers—have strutted this sea-set stage. Wars and expeditions have been planned, and sieges sustained ; while explorers, merchant venturers and founders of new Englands have taken their last look at the mother country from vessels riding in the Sound. On the authority of Leland we gather that in the reign of Henry the Second this place was " a mene thing as an inhabitation for fishers." By the middle of the thirteenth century it had grown to such importance that a market was added to its amenities, and some years later a fleet of three hundred and more vessels sailed from hence to Guienne. A petition dated 1414 describes Plymouth as a great port for the harbour of vessels and speaks of the weak defences of the town, calling attention to its frequent destruction by the enemy in time of war. From the middle of the fourteenth century to the beginning of the fifteenth it was subject to frequent attacks from the French, but such was the tenacity of the townspeople that the

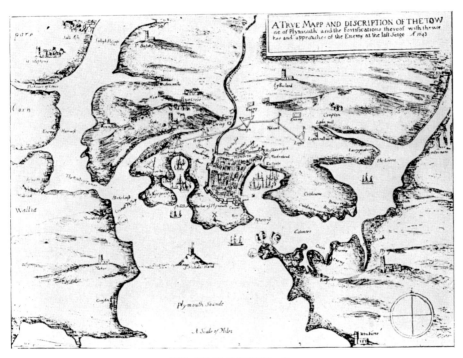

MAP OF PLYMOUTH. 1643.

place quickly recovered from all assaults. An Act of Parliament was passed in 1512 for fortifying Plymouth and other seaport towns. A chart of the town drawn in the reign of Henry the Eighth is preserved in the British Museum, showing the topography of the place and the chief buildings, as it doubtless appeared when Leland made his inspection and wrote " the mouth of the Gulph, where the shippers of Plymouth lyith is waullid on eche side and chained over in tyme of necessitie." From this chart, drawn in crude perspective, the churches of Plymouth and Stonehouse can be traced ; they have been placed with considerable accuracy, and it is interesting to note are still in situ. The foreshore is fortified and cannon project from embrasures to guard the Cattewater and the entrance to the Hamoaze at Stonehouse. Even the chain is shown stretched across Sutton Pool. The disposition

E

of mediæval Plymouth appears from this chart to have centred between the two parish churches. Stonehouse is shown as an independent township protected by fortifications, while the site of Devonport is open country (page 48). The aspect of the town could have changed but little when Drake sailed forth on his expedition to Nombre de Dios in 1572, to return a year later, but it had grown in size when he was elected mayor in 1582, and the wealth of the citizens can be adjudged from the

MAP OF PLYMOUTH. 1758.

rich carvings and external appearance of the timber houses that still watch the doings in the streets near the Barbican. Great was the excitement when the Armada was sighted off the port on July 20th, 1588, and eager were the preparations on board the fleet of one hundred and ninety ships collected here to resist the invaders. Plymouth a few years later became the centre for projects in connection with the planting of colonies in North America, and a " Plymouth Company " was sanctioned by James the First. In 1620 the *Mayflower* set sail with its precious freight of pilgrims. When Charles the First visited Plymouth in 1625 the town still clustered about the harbour, and although several new fortifications had been added it had not perceptibly increased in size.

During the period of the Civil War the Parliamentary forces held the town, even when the whole of the West of England was occupied by the Royalists. The first siege of Plymouth was undertaken soon after the beginning of the war, and in 1643 Colonel Digby was sent with a considerable force to reduce the place, but failed in his enterprise, for the siege was raised on the 25th of October. In the same year " A True Mapp and Description of the Towne of Plymouth and the fortifications thereof and the works and approaches of the enemy at the last siege " was published (page 49). This map is interesting as it shows the position of the forts and the outer protection works, together with the leet called Sir Francis Drake's Water, from whence the town drew its water supply. From April 14th, 1644, to the 10th of January, 1646, the town again underwent the rigours of siege and blockade, but such was the stoutness of the defence that even the presence of the monarch could not aid his troops in the attack and the siege was abandoned, but the struggle cost the inhabitants a loss of eight thousand lives. This failure so impressed Charles the Second that one of his first undertakings after the Restoration was to order the building of a citadel so strong that the townspeople should be overawed and deterred from ever again attempting to dispute the royal authority. After the building of

MAP OF PLYMOUTH DOCK (DEVONPORT). 1811.

the Citadel the town expanded slightly to the west and north, but otherwise was found convenient to the needs of the population.

Sutton Pool was at this time thought inadequate as an anchorage for great ships, which perforce had to ride in the Sound, no secure place during gales, and when the necessity for a west-country naval centre appeared desirable, after the Revolution of 1688, a Royal Dockyard was inaugurated on the east bank of the Hamoaze, beyond Stonehouse. The yard was first named Plymouth Yard, and the houses that sprang up about it Plymouth Dock. Vanbrugh was called upon by the Admiralty to design the original gun wharf and the brick house for the Commissioner which is still in existence. Devonport, as this place came to be known after 1820, when the name was changed by Royal Charter, will be discussed later. A map of 1758 (page 50) shows the relation of Plymouth to the Citadel; it will also be seen on reference to this map that the mediæval streets were extended in a northerly direction, as certain of the townspeople at this period desired to live on the outskirts of the town rather than near the centre, which was becoming crowded. Many of the picturesque brick houses facing the Barbican belong to the early years of the eighteenth century. These were built to accommodate the merchants and others who wished to supervise the lading of their vessels in Sutton Pool. After 1750 numerous other improvements took place, such as the straightening of certain streets by substituting brick-fronted and stone-built houses for the overhanging

MAP OF DEVONPORT. 1820.

timber fronts characteristic of the sixteenth and seventeenth centuries. The change in the aspect of the town can be followed from a study of contemporary prints in the Cottonian Library and the Municipal Gallery. During the second half of the eighteenth century the growth of Plymouth was in the direction of Plymouth Marsh and Millbay, as the houses in George Street testify. But in the meantime Plymouth Dock was developing almost to the dimensions of the old town, and Stonehouse, shorn of its mediæval aspect, assumed the genteel costume of the late period, and Durnford Street with Emma Place, a representative and excellent piece of town planning of the time, became the residential centre for admirals and other naval officers of high rank. Thus three important links in the chain of towns were almost ready to be connected. Such was the aspect of Plymouth in 1815 when Napoleon, from the deck of the *Bellerophon*, first surveyed the naval port at close quarters. The map of Plymouth Dock drawn up in 1811 (page 51) is interesting on two counts, for it shows how the proximity of the Dockyard and the Gun Wharf brought about the formation of the streets of the Dockyard township, and determined the placing of the markets and other public centres. After the granting of the charter of 1820, when the name was changed to Devonport, a further map was published, but this does not provide any additional information as to the growth of the place during the interval of fourteen years. We are, however, not concerned so much with the development of the individual townships as with the growth of Plymouth as a whole, and for this purpose the plan of the Towns and Harbour of Plymouth, Stonehouse, Devonport, Morice Town, and Stoke, published in 1825, offers the best index of the state of the district when George the Fourth was king. Plymouth and Devonport were bound to gravitate toward their meta-centre, Stonehouse, which at the end of the eighteenth century harboured the aristocratic population who directed the industry of the Dockyard, and extended their patronage to the tradespeople of both places. This growth was inevitable, it was logical, and moreover it was, within certain bounds, sure. But the growth might have been allowed to spread without control but for the genius of a man who grasped all the

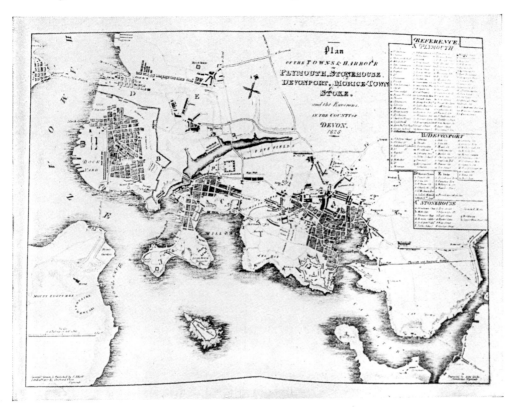

MAP OF THE THREE TOWNS IN 1825.

possibilities of the district, and left his stamp upon the architecture of the West of England. John Foulston was a London man who had been a pupil in Thomas Hardwick's office. In 1812 he competed for the new hotel and theatre projected for Plymouth. His design was accepted and in consequence he took up his residence in the town. Land in those days was cheap, architects were few, and builders were eager to speculate. The result was that this architect soon became the master of ceremonies in all that pertained to the amenities of the three towns. His first care was to project a new road from George Street, Plymouth, to Stonehouse, to serve as a main arterial communication.

The map of 1825 shows this road partially completed on the Stonehouse side,

E *

but passing between open land across Plymouth Marsh. Foulston, like Grainger, of Newcastle, was fired with the desire to emulate Nash's work in London ; the moment and the man had arrived for such developments, and the result was the shaping of Union Street with the Octagon as a hiatus at the centre. Foulston's other town-planning achievements included Athenæum Street, Lockyer Street, the Crescent and a range of villas called Devonshire Villas to the north of the town. In addition to designing the majority of the terraces in Plymouth he constructed nearly all the public buildings, with the exception of the Customs House, which was designed by Laing ; and he at this time prepared plans for nearly all the minor streets which the speculative builders of the day were eager to proceed with. Plymouth in the early 'twenties was a forest of scaffold poles, soon to be cleared to reveal the stuccoed conventions in Greek taste devised by this architect. It is, of course, burking the question to assume that Foulston designed every house, but his personality is stamped on the doors, windows and iron gates, while it is clear the builders of the time were sworn to allegiance, for they caught the spirit of his manner and faithfully obeyed his orders. At Stoke Damerel, Foulston's hand is to be seen in the composition of the stately façade forming St. Michael's Terrace, as well as in the unique Albemarle Villas which are contiguous. His work at Devonport included the civic centre, the Naval Column and many other works. He occasionally lapsed into Hindoo and Gothic of his own invention, but the generality of his work is free from eccentricity, and compares favourably with contemporary practice in London.

To catalogue all the works of this man would require a special index, therefore it is sufficient for the purposes of this book to say that the real linking up to Plymouth and the neighbouring towns took place between 1812 and 1830. Cooke's new plan of the three towns of Plymouth, Devonport, and Stonehouse, published in 1844, at the close of Foulston's career (when he took Wightwick as a partner), shows to what an extent Plymouth had extended by the middle of the last century. Wightwick belonged to the Italian school, and although he profited by Foulston's teachings he allowed his pencil to run riot among bay windows and heavy balconies with no sparing touch ; but even as late as 1860 the value of the Foulston tradition was understood by local builders. Wightwick's best architectural work is perhaps the range of houses forming a composition of three masses, known as the Esplanade, on the Hoe. Wightwick had a great deal to do with the new buildings in Devonport which were erected after 1850, and he refronted the Plymouth Library and Cottonian Museum, previously designed by Foulston. Reference to the modern plan of Plymouth proves what a steadying influence the town planning of the Regency period exerted upon the later development—important not only for the link it provides in the natural growth of Plymouth, but ensuring the right character to the district immediately surrounding the Hoe, and functional as an extension of the old town. In the 'thirties only prosperous people could afford a town house in this fashionable district, but time works many changes and superior boarding establishments and private hotels now occupy the rooms once frequented by personages connected with the naval dockyards and the garrison. When Brunel took the Railway on to Plymouth from Exeter he incorporated into the new system the existing " Atmospheric Railway " and ensured direct communication with London. This event was followed with the extension of the line across the Tamar at Saltash. At a later date North Road station was built, but it is a pleasant crinoline structure and one reflecting its period. From 1860 to the present time new suburbs have been added in various outlying parts, practically without cessation. Morice Town is already double the size of its neighbour, Devonport ; Stoke has thrown out tentacles, while to the north, Mutley is spreading with the virility of a disease. East of Sutton Pool on either side of Friary Station a colony of small houses covering a site three times the extent of that occupied by the mediæval town marks the most recent industrial development, and Plymouth is still increasing. The growing pains of the modern

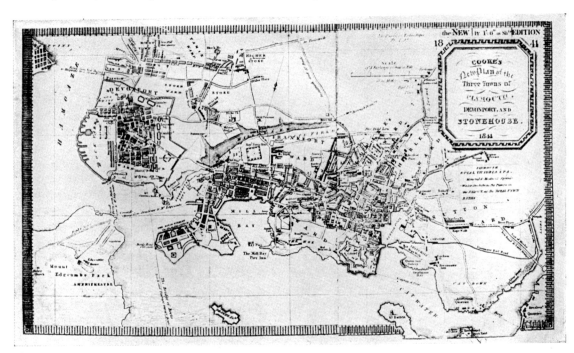

COOKE'S NEW PLAN OF THE THREE TOWNS. 1844.

parts of the three towns could have been obviated had a town-planning scheme on the right lines been laid down ten years ago. It is not too late even at this juncture to remedy the defects, for the natural situation of this untitular capital, with its unique advantages of communication by road and water, materially strengthens such aims.

No one can visit Plymouth without carrying away haunting memories of the place. For this historic port is a centre to the earth, from whence vessels sail to America and Japan, and from whence grey battleships issue to protect the coasts of this and other lands. Every Plymouth emigrant retains some impressive vision of the mist, some aspect of the setting sun over the Cornish hills, some thought of the frowning countenance of Dartmoor, some remembrance of Union Street with its perspective of lamps and throngs of soldiers and sailors. Such scenes are indelibly stamped in the mind. The writer knows the place, although he cannot claim to be a native; he has tramped its streets and found comfort from the facial aspect of its buildings, he has admired the marble of its pavements, and has partaken of the hospitality of its people.

MONUMENTAL ARCHITECTURE AT PLYMOUTH

Plymouth with its historical associations is the product of centuries; it is allied to the sea, upon which it relies for sustenance and protection much as a capital

DEVONPORT DOCKYARD AND THE TAMAR FROM MOUNT EDGCUMBE.
Early nineteenth century.

city depends upon its river. No definite plan attended the birth of this western port; it has grown to meet the needs of the Navy.

Devonport, as this place came to be known later by Royal Charter after 1820, contains many eighteenth-century examples of minor importance. After the year 1750 many alterations took place; certain old streets were straightened by the substitution of brick-fronted houses in place of the projecting timber fronts characteristic of the sixteenth and seventeenth centuries. To this period belonged the old Marine Barracks, Stonehouse, demolished when Durnford Street was constructed, a stone-fronted Palladian building strongly reminiscent of the façade to the Ironmongers' Hall. Then was built (in 1762) the Royal Naval Hospital, Stonehouse,

ROYAL NAVAL HOSPITAL, STONEHOUSE. THE ENTRANCE. 1810.

THE NAVAL HOSPITAL, STONEHOUSE. 1770–1775.
Formerly the Administrative Block.

probably from plans by William Robinson, the style of the building being remarkably similar to this architect's work in London.

The entrance gates to the hospital courtyard (see page 57) belong to the early years of the nineteenth century. The simplicity of the iron grilles, the character of the lamps and the supports, together with the excellent carvings in relief by R. Smith, will be of special interest to designers. The grouping of the original buildings can be seen through the grille.

From the courtyard, looking due west, will be seen the block of buildings, formerly the Administrative Department to the Hospital (see page 58), the centre portion of the group being in brickwork and the side groups (of early nineteenth-century date) in stone. There is strong reason for assuming these subordinate buildings to have been designed by Alexander, who may well have been responsible for the gate piers and the grille. We can leave the discussion of the monumental buildings of the seaport for a space to continue with facts concerning the further development of the town. It is evident that the second half of the eighteenth century witnessed the growth of Plymouth in the direction of Plymouth Marsh and Millbay, as can be seen from the style of the fine brick houses in George Street, some of which retain their elegant wooden cornices. In the meantime Plymouth Dock was developing almost to the dimensions of the old town. Stonehouse, sandwiched between the Dock and the seaport, became the fashionable residential centre for the families of naval officers. Then ensued a demand for new houses and in consequence Durnford Street and Emma Place record the excellent town developments of those days.

Plymouth differs from all other English towns by the feeling she inspires ; she is naval from first to last. It is true that great liners make Plymouth a port of call, that the overseas mails arrive and depart by express train ; but such things are mere interludes in the vast task of providing for the needs of the Navy.

Granted the necessity of a fleet, the problem is its equipment ; and of equal importance is the feeding of the personnel. While Foulston was doing something to better the appearance of the seaport on the land side, even by the manipulation of speculative builders, the Admiralty determined upon a work of national importance, namely, building a breakwater across Plymouth Sound. This work was started in 1813, and completed ten years later, under many difficulties. It is estimated that five and a half million tons of granite were deposited. The plans for this work were prepared by Joseph Whidby. It was, however, left to Mr. (afterwards Sir) John Rennie to complete the work. Here is an extract from his exceedingly modest account : " The next great work was the finishing of the great breakwater in Plymouth Sound. The chief merit I claim for this is in adding the benching or beam on the outside, at the base of the sea slope, which breaks the sea before it reaches the slope and prevents it from acting injuriously upon it. I also claim a certain portion of the credit for arranging and executing the paving of the upper surface and the dovetailed masonry of the two ends of the breakwater."

To this personal account of a work of architectural engineering can be added the fact that Rennie was responsible for the design of the lighthouse on the Plymouth Breakwater, and for other features making for character, both efficient and ornamental.

THE ROYAL VICTUALLING YARD, STONEHOUSE. 1830. (General view, showing grouping).
Sir John Rennie, Architect.

THE ROYAL VICTUALLING YARD, STONEHOUSE. CENTRAL BLOCK AND WINGS.
Sir John Rennie, Architect.

THE ROYAL VICTUALLING YARD, STONEHOUSE. THE ENTRANCE. 1830.
Sir John Rennie, Architect.

The average architect with leanings towards the achievements of foreigners is apt to think that the finest schemes belong to the other side of the Channel. Such opinions do not take into account the vast architectural engineering conception realised by men of the status of John Rennie during the first quarter of the last century. Such a scheme as the Victualling Yard at Stonehouse, complete down to the design of the lamp-posts, conceived on the grand scale, directly stating its purpose, traditional, yet original, free from fashion, but as modern to-day as it will be centuries hence, deserves to be recognised among the monuments of this country.

Sir John Rennie does not enter into detailed accounts of this work. He says : " The design and execution of the Royal William Victualling Establishment at Stonehouse, near Devonport, I claim entirely as my own, with the exception of the machinery, for which my brother George is entitled to an equal share of the credit with myself." " This establishment, including the cost of the land, amounted, I believe, to between £600,000 and £700,000." To-day it would cost nearly five millions.

Viewed from across the Hamoaze, the grouping of the buildings consists of three main blocks. The centre block is recessed to form the head of the basin (see page 60). In length and general massing the centre building corresponds to the scale of the Customs House at Dublin. It has no claim to complex richness, neither is it ornate, but from one end to the other, from the water-line to the vane on the cupola, it expresses its purpose. The effect of breadth, rhythm, mass and scale is attained by direct statement of fact, together with a masterly knowledge of material and technique. The building is monumental in scale, there is an entire absence of frippery and meretricious ornament. This façade contains the proportions of an order which is conspicuous by its absence. The theme is Doric in its main idea, but of a Spartan severity in opposition to Athenian grace.

Very few architects of the period would have dared to treat the silhouette of this building as Rennie has done. Laing, the architect of the Customs House in London, could not have done it. Alexander never had the opportunity ; Cockerell, Rennie's brother-in-law, was too much in love with sculpturesque architecture. We are confronted with a curious example of engineer's architecture, academic to a degree, related to the whole sequence of the English tradition as far as grouping, fenestration and style are concerned, inheriting to some extent the fanciful outline of contemporary French works of similar character—for example, those illustrated by Gourlier—but as a building, fulfilling all the laws of taste and reflecting in an abstract way the personality and power of the architect-engineer. Sir John Rennie had no need to write a full description of his works. They stand to-day as he left them, not a stone out of place, not a slate loose, mellowed by the weather and fulfilling their purpose.

Viewed from the quay the buildings group well in steep perspective, there is no forced effect about them. Here the cupola comes into the picture from a different aspect to soften and foil the gigantic masses of masonry. The younger Dance handled the masonry of Newgate in the humour of Piranesi. His was the task and opportunity to impart character to a prison in the centre of London, a comparatively small problem compared to the task of Rennie, who had to design a structure capable of holding its own amidst a vast expanse of natural scenery.

[THE ROYAL VICTUALLING YARD, STONEHOUSE. 1830 (Main Buildings in steep perspective, looking towards Entrance Gateway).
Sir John Rennie, Architect.

ROYAL NAVAL HOSPITAL, STONEHOUSE. OFFICE BUILDING.
Early nineteenth century.

THE ROYAL NAVAL HOSPITAL, STONEHOUSE. ENTRANCE GROUP.

The approaches to the Yard are bad—a fault that is notoriously common in England. From the sea there is no impediment; cutter and pinnace, yawl and lighter, enter the basin direct from the Hamoaze. From the land side the tale is different; first, one has to find Durnford Street, and then by devious lanes one approaches the main gate, which is boldly conceived, but marred by the absurd figure of King William the Fourth, the one solecism in the design (see page 63).

THE ROYAL VICTUALLING YARD, STONEHOUSE.
GARDEN SEAT. 1830.

Rennie could on occasion devise minor features of character; the lamp-posts in the yard are his, also the roomy garden seats. His main forte, however, was the treatment of masonry, the carrying to completion of projects vast in scale, and the solving of problems outside the scope of ordinary practice.

The construction of the Victualling Yard necessitated the use of the diving bell, the foundation of the sea-wall being laid eleven feet below watermark. When it is remembered that the architect-engineer not only prepared the design but settled all matters relating to construction and the invention of appliances for the expedition and carrying out of works, some idea of the work involved may be formed. Sir John Rennie had little time for architectural training. He was forced to confine himself to civil engineering. Acquaintance with his father's scheme for Waterloo, London, and Southwark bridges, upon which he worked and one of which he finished, gave him the necessary insight into the working and handling of masonry. Holyhead, Kingstown, and Ramsgate harbours provided him with scope for his energies. In those days architects and engineers were always at school; few designers thought of practising without a library of works relating to their profession; a fact made clear when the names in the volumes at the Institute of Civil Engineers are consulted. The conditions of early nineteenth-century building on the grand scale demanded direct statement. The country understood the value of straightforward

ROYAL NAVAL HOSPITAL, STONEHOUSE.
SUNDIAL IN QUADRANGLE. 1770.

F

THE BALL-ROOM, ROYAL HOTEL, PLYMOUTH.
John Foulston, Architect.

architecture; mere prettiness would not suffice for naval affairs, hence the opportunity afforded to Rennie by the Admiralty and the completion of the yard, quay, basin, bridges, and houses forming the vast establishment at Plymouth.

PLYMOUTH (*Minor Buildings*)

There is another aspect of the building traditions of Plymouth and Devonport which is no less essential to a comprehensive account of the town's architecture. In the main the buildings are the result of the extraordinary versatility and herculean

THE PROPRIETARY LIBRARY, PLYMOUTH.

labours of John Foulston. There is, for example, the Royal Hotel and the Theatre (see page 18), which externally present a combination grouping unaltered since the date of erection. At the Royal Hotel there is a splendid ball-room which can be accounted to be one of Foulston's best works. This room was designed in 1806–7. The lighting by lunette windows which entered the segmental ceiling is most satisfactory. The ornate design of the musicians' gallery is peculiarly English. Reference to the illustration of the latter feature will show the skill of the designer in devising the console supports which diminish in projecting to suit the soft curvature of the balcony. Another of Foulston's achievements was the building of the Proprietary Library, in which the architect had recourse to Soanean methods of lighting ; this

THE PROPRIETARY LIBRARY, PLYMOUTH. VIEW OF READING-ROOM. *John Foulston, Architect.*
This is rightly considered to be Foulston's best work.

THE PROPRIETARY LIBRARY, PLYMOUTH. THE LANTERN.
John Foulston, Architect.

ROYAL HOTEL, PLYMOUTH. DETAIL OF BALCONY IN BALL-ROOM.
John Foulston, Architect.

F *

library he finished in 1809. The illustrations include an engraving by Wilson, a detail of the circular lantern and a general view showing the treatment of the internal angles and the galleries. The view of the exterior records the alteration made to the façade by Wightwick to replace Foulston's plain front. The design as altered lacks the simple grace of Foulston's work, but it is strong and the disposition of the windows is admirable. It should be noted how the large windows blend harmoniously with those of smaller size above, the junction being effected by means of the balustraded balconies of slight projection. Another of Foulston's minor essays is the

DEVON AND CORNWALL FEMALE ORPHANAGE, LOCKYER STREET, PLYMOUTH.
Foulston and Wightwick, Architects.

Naval Column at Devonport which, together with the municipal buildings, forms one of the chief attributes of the civic centre. The column is one of the few monuments erected at the beginning of the last century to commemorate the triumphs of the Navy over the French fleet. One of Foulston's later works, The Devon and Cornwall Female Orphanage in Lockyer Street, was the joint work of Foulston and Wightwick; it was completed in 1834. As a simple and straightforward design, free from adventitious ornament, it is in marked contrast to the vulgar tendencies which in some quarters spoil direct expression to-day.

Foulston will be best remembered for his town domestic work which covers almost every type of house, from the terrace groupings of Wyndham Square to the

ST. MICHAEL'S LODGE, STOKE DAMEREL, DEVONPORT.
Early nineteenth century. *John Foulston, Architect.*

No. 2 ALBERMARLE VILLAS, STOKE DAMEREL.
Typical " Regency " Villa. *John Foulston, Architect.*

THE ESPLANADE, PLYMOUTH HOE. 1836.
Wightwick, Architect.

MOUNT WISE, DEVONPORT. GROUP OF SMALL HOUSES.
Late eighteenth century.

austere range of houses forming St. Michael's Terrace at Stoke Damerel. Foulston, in emulation of John Nash, had a true appreciation of scale, he realised that impressive dignity for the residential quarters of a town could only result from pleasant formality. In detail most of Foulston's work is heavy, but he never loses touch with the requirements of human scale and proportion. Not only did Foulston prepare schemes for the speculative builders of the time, but he devised many attractive villas to suit private clients. St. Michael's Lodge at Stoke Damerel is an excellent example of this architect's skill. At the beginning of the nineteenth century Stoke Damerel was a suburb of Devonport, and at this date proved more attractive as a residential

ST. BONIFACE'S COLLEGE, WYNDHAM SQUARE, PLYMOUTH. 1835.
John Foulston, Architect.

centre than Stonehouse. The illustration, No. 2 Albemarle Villas, Stoke Damerel (page 71), is typical of Foulston's Regency manner. It is a replica in miniature of the larger houses of the time. All the villas vary in form and detail; the interior arrangements include geometrical staircases, marble fireplaces and plaster cornices of precise classic stamp.

While Foulston and Wightwick were in full practice a very distinguished architect visited Plymouth in the person of Professor Cockerell, who in the position of architect to the Bank of England was commissioned to remodel the western branch of the Bank. It is a simple example of the taste of this pre-eminently classic mind. Cockerell had to consider adapting an existing building; the problem being

THE BANK OF ENGLAND, PLYMOUTH. 1835.
Professor C. R. Cockerell, R.A., Architect.

ST. MICHAEL'S TERRACE, STOKE DAMEREL, PLYMOUTH.
John Foulston, Architect.

THE PROPRIETARY LIBRARY, PLYMOUTH, AS REFRONTED BY WIGHTWICK.

THE CUSTOMS HOUSE, PLYMOUTH. 1810.

David Laing, Architect.

to design new banking premises on the ground floor. To accomplish this the architect introduced an arcuated treatment in which Florentine rustications form the chief feature.

From 1840 to 1850 the style of Foulston was continued by his partner Wightwick, but it gradually became more complex in expression and eventually tailed off into a species of Italian viewed through Victorian spectacles ; finally becoming dull and colourless. Notwithstanding the decline from the Spartan severity of the Regency period, Plymouth builders never entirely lost touch with the teachings of Foulston, to whom the town is indebted for the orderly arrangement of the streets and the homogeneity of the terraces.

THE NAVAL COLUMN,
DEVONPORT.
John Foulston, Architect.

CHAPTER IV

THE DEVELOPMENT OF THE REGIONAL TRADITION DESCRIBED IN DETAIL, INFLUENCES ANALYSED, MATERIALS USED

NATIVE METHODS PRIOR TO CLASSICAL DEVELOPMENT—17TH CENTURY FORMATIVE PERIOD (1600–1730)

NO other country but England can show in its historic buildings how the interests of the people have centred about home life. It is in this particular, as well as in the slight changes that mark the sustained process of transition from the fancies of one generation to another, that the main interest of the subject centres. The west country is particularly rich in such

THE MARKET HOUSE, ASHBURTON, DEVON.
Late sixteenth century.

associations, and on this count the buildings of the people not only serve as an index to historical facts, but by strength of lineament and functional presentment demonstrate the native facility for intentional structure. For many reasons it is not possible to enter upon the early history of building in Devon and Cornwall. It is, however, safe to assume that centuries of tradition in the art and craft of masonry, as exemplified in the magnificent churches and towers of mediæval times, had produced its counterpart in castles, manors and town houses. This interest in turn gave place to the Tudor phase, when mediæval instincts broadened and became more receptive to the spirit of freedom engendered by the Reformation. Finally, we come to the period of the late sixteenth century when the theory of a house being a home and not a fortified stronghold had gained common acceptance and was in practice to suit the needs of the social scale.

At the time of the Armada large houses were built in country and town almost exclusively for the pleasure of the occupant. This influence reacted on the homes of the people, as was to be expected, and so there came about the long and low farm-house with its roof of thatch and stepped chimney-stacks ; the walls of cob or stone, roughly squared, with mullioned windows of wood or stone, its massive walls, deep recesses and flagged kitchen. A development related to the sumptuous scale and finish of, to name examples, Bradninch Manor House, of Sydenham House, with its gabled silhouette, of the richly ornate front to the Guildhall at Exeter, as well as Trerice in Cornwall and the old stone houses at Tintagel, Boscastle, and Stratton. The west country was the stronghold of the seafaring Elizabethans, as it was the centre of the woolstapling industry which, with the rise of sea power, left East Anglia and came westwards. The adventurous spirit that permeated all classes of society at this time is clearly shown in the buildings, for it is evident that pains and skill were not spared to produce work both pleasing to the eye and sound in construction. As regards planning the larger houses conform to the Elizabethan practice of regularity, while those of humbler size and less pretension inherit the earlier mediæval dispositions, changed to suit individual tastes and local circumstances. It is im-

EXE ISLAND, EXETER. SIXTEENTH-CENTURY HOUSE, WITH EARLY SLATE SHINGLING.

possible to pass such works without being struck by the element of freshness in the grouping as well as noting the artistry displayed in fashioning the silhouette of the ensemble, and the high artistic sense exhibited in the accent and finish given to door, window, and chimney-stack. To this period of well building, when the selection of site was all-important, both as regards proximity to a quarry and manorial and agricultural considerations, can be attributed the culmination of those regional influences which constitute the Spartan principles of functional expression underlying the architecture of the western region. Almost every hamlet

ALMSHOUSES, MORETONHAMPSTEAD.
STONE AND THATCH. 1637.

and village in Devon and Cornwall possesses a specimen or so of the building of this and earlier times ; the work collectively is more rightly distinguished by the term building, for its artistic qualities almost defy analysis ; it has the merit of the picturesque which is the despair of modern attainment, it shows errors of detail that mark it out as being something above rules and formalities. In a word, it is building, simple, unaffected and practically unfettered. At the opening of the seventeenth century, when the mediæval accent in externals was yielding to the warming influence of the classic stream, there ensued a fusion of ideas, both local and foreign, which masons and carpenters dealt with with extraordinary aptitude. The Tudor house on Exe Island in the city of Exeter exhibits some curious contrasts in general disposition, it is related to many of the timber-framed houses, the storeys of which overhang the older quarters. It is, moreover, especially noteworthy by reason of the interesting detail of its slate shingling, which for three and a half centuries has adhered to the original battening.

Another interesting group is that of the Almshouses, Moretonhampstead, which belongs to the early seventeenth century. Here the influence is directly and unmistakably Italian. The loggia-like treatment to the ground storey blends harmoniously with the fenestration over and the steep-pitched thatch roof. The finish of the chimney-stacks, on the other hand, accords with Tudor practice (see illustration above).

Further evidence of the early-tradition, mediæval and Tudor, is afforded by the stone and slate

THE OLD GUILDHALL, TOTNES, DEVON. STONE AND SLATE PLEASANTLY USED. Early seventeenth century.

BRADNINCH MANOR HOUSE, BRADNINCH, DEVON.
Original house, late sixteenth century. Centre portion added after 1730.

ASHBURTON, DEVON.
General view of houses in North Street.

externals of the Old Guildhall at Totnes (page 80). Bradninch Manor House, built in the sixteenth century, both as regards plan and external treatment, as well as the character of the interior joinery, expresses the high-level achievement of local Elizabethans. Here the walls are of stone, but the mullions, frames, and transomes to the older windows are of wood. About the year 1730 a portion of the Manor House was destroyed by fire, thus accounting for the reconstruction of the garden front to accord with the mode fashionable during the reign of George the Second.

HOUSES, ASHBURTON, DEVON.
Showing types of slate hanging. Late seventeenth century.

We have now to turn to the town of Ashburton on the river Yeo, the waters of which flow through the town and in the old days drove the mills. Here the houses are constructed with the stone of the locality and in some cases overhung with slate obtained from neighbouring quarries. In ancient times the people derived its prosperity from the tin and copper mines and, at a later date, the town became important as a woolstapling centre. The houses for the most part are commodious and show the importance of those who worked and lived within the precincts. To-day it has fallen from its seventeenth-century industrial status and prosperity to the somnolence of a grave country town, awakening, it is true, to a sense of its former activity on market days, but notwithstanding its decline and settlement of an interest that is unforgettable. Two illustrations are given of typical Ashburton houses of the late seventeenth century. The gable, both single and M-shaped, is the outstanding feature, but the charm inheres in the informality of the composition of details, such as the modillion cornice, the heavily sashed windows and the slate hanging with its varieties of texture and patterning.

HOUSE IN HIGH STREET, EXETER.
Pivot type, showing full Dutch influence. Late seventeenth century.

To the last quarter of the seventeenth century, as pointed out in the preceding chapter and in the description of Exeter, can be assigned the minor reverberations of the Dutch style which entered the west country direct from Holland. The former seaport of Topsham appears to have been the principal entry. At this time the woolstapling industry, carried on so successfully at Tiverton, Honiton and other towns in Devon as well as in the city of Exeter, resulted in direct trading from the western capital to Holland. Prior to the accession to the throne of England of William of Orange and his consort Mary, Topsham was the principal seaport for the towns of mid and South Devon that traded with the Continent. In consequence a few Exeter merchants built houses near the quays of the seaport in order to expedite their business affairs. The house with the curvilinear gable is selected for illustration as an instance of the contemporary taste for ideas out of the Netherlands. As Topsham assumed a greater prosperity, so Exeter, the parent city, grew jealous of her diminutive offspring. Recourse was therefore made to the ingenuity of certain Dutchmen skilled in the fashioning of canals, and to the subsequent improving of the Exe canal for navigation by comparatively large vessels can be assigned the pronounced influence of Dutch ideas and the prevalence of Anglo-Dutch ornament and detail in Exeter itself.

The house in High Street, Exeter, fronting Queen Street, is one of the most important in the latter regard. In design it is as complete as a tall Dutch cabinet, including the full cornice and the meticulous inlaying of brick detail, such as the minor panels, ellipsoids and segmental pediment. This house is now held by the firm of Gould and Allen, who took over the premises in 1803. There are many illustrations of façades in Vingboon's book that show similar treatments. When first built this house sported the traditional mullioned and transomed windows with lead glazing; the present sashed windows belong to the close of the eighteenth century. No other house of the period 1690-1700 in the city of Exeter demonstrates the angle of Dutch incidence more clearly than this interesting example. It is at once an index to local enterprise and proof positive of the many sources from which contemporary art was drawn. At this period Sir Christopher Wren and his contemporaries were moulding the style in the main, but the broader issues of regional expansion and development belongs, and rightly belongs, to the enterprise of the people who desired houses and the skill of local craftsmen who carried out the ideas. On such counts and more it is just to consider this house to be a pivot type upon which many others in the district were based.

HOUSE, FORE STREET, EXETER. 1702.

Another example chosen for illustration, this time from Fore Street, Exeter, is conspicuous for its personality. Built about the year 1702 it combines in its brick treatment distinct traits influenced from buildings in Holland as well as the best qualities of local craftsmanship. Both this example and the one previously discussed replaced timber-framed houses of mediæval style. The house in Fore Street has the additional interest of revealing how cross currents of building style were affecting the western vernacular. In the first place, the builder had the task of fronting an existing Tudor house; in the second, he had to devise a comparatively plain front of local brickwork which fashion, imitating London ways, was demanding; he was also confronted with Dutch ideas and not a little perplexed regarding the vertical sequence of the windows. His native skill and unerring instinct for the essentials of composition forced him, perhaps subconsciously, to combine Jacobean interest with Dutch loquacity, the result being a most fascinating and successful *tour de force*. Such are a few of the truths revealed in the aspect of the minor house-fronts of Exeter, particularly those built at the close of the seventeenth and the beginning of the eighteenth century.

G *

Reverting to Topsham at the time of its prosperity, a further development of the vernacular is to be seen in the Salutation Inn, famous as an hostelry for travellers by road from North to South Devon as well as a rest-house for those travelling by sea to the Continent. This building which, in its external treatment as in the interior details of the Assembly Room and other apartments, follows the mode of 1720, marks another and later stage of the formative development. By this time the Dutch influence had become completely anglicised. The main feature of the design is the prominence given to the Assembly Room, which is placed over the coach entrance and in former days was supported on two timber Doric columns of proved substance. The original stone pedestals are in situ, but the corpulent supports have in the last twenty years been replaced by modern brick piers which lack grace and character, apart from their efficiency as structural supports.

THE SALUTATION INN, TOPSHAM, DEVON. 1720.

The concentration of building interest within the city of Exeter during the closing years of the seventeenth and the opening years of the eighteenth century reveals diverse interests and aspirations, local, foreign and national, which collectively make up the regional aspect of the formative development. There are evidences of a parallel development in the neighbouring towns of Cullompton and Tiverton, which owes its features as much to the trend of building traditions advancing westwards through the fair counties, by way of Bath and Bristol, as it does to the exemplars afforded by the building of great houses for the nobility. The work of this time accords with types found in Oxfordshire, Berkshire, Somerset, and Dorset. It is true that in every particular the detail corresponds to what had by this time become common practice in the treatment of stone and brick in every part of the country ; a semi-standardisation of type made possible by the labours of Sir Christopher Wren, his contemporaries and successors. But contact with the western region brought about specific changes in expression, traditions of craftsmanship were not to be changed in a moment. As a result many buildings of the early eighteenth century inherit tendencies already out of fashion in the metropolis ; a point worthy of consideration, for to some extent it explains the peculiar charm and freshness of handling never absent from the west-country home.

We have now to turn to Barnstaple, Appledore, and Bideford, the northern centres of Devon, places that formed integral assets in the course of Elizabethan adventure and in the seventeenth century, thanks to the development of the shipping interest on the north coast, were no mean competitors with Plymouth. Barnstaple can show some interesting doorways of the early period. Butcher's Row and the Market afford evidence of the activity of commercial life of the time. There is the ornate Queen Anne's Walk with the chubby figure of the queen in stone at the centre. Appledore reflects Barnstaple in miniature. The chief distinction, therefore, rests with Bideford—or By-the-Ford—a town picturesquely placed at the foot of a hill and divided unequally by the river Torridge. An index to the former prosperity of the town is forthcoming in the Corporation insignia and maces of

28 BRIDGELAND STREET, BIDEFORD. 1691-1693.
Nathaniel Gascoyne, Architect.

Elizabethan and Carolean fashioning. There is the silver one formerly belonging to the Lord of the Manor, and the mayor's chain, which consists of thirty-five links of gold. There are the ancient seals, the oldest of which bears the device of the bridge of which the town is justly proud. Bideford is a place of romantic associations. It was the home of Sir Richard Grenville, it has entertained Sir Joshua Reynolds and Dr. Johnson, it was familiar to John Gay, and has been immortalised by Kingsley.

In the later years of the seventeenth century Bideford reached the zenith of its prosperity and maintained its status until the second half of the eighteenth century. It owed its rise to the growth of the American plantations, and the maintenance of its consequence to trade with the New World. Further proof in this regard is forthcoming in the fact that for close on two centuries most of the tobacco consumed in this country was imported from America and passed through the town. The problem of surplus tobacco hogsheads was happily solved in 1673, when difficulties experienced in dealing with refuse from the houses were met by an order issued to the inhabitants to the effect that all refuse was to be deposited in tobacco hogsheads provided by the authorities for the use of houses in certain streets. From 1660 onwards trade began to thrive, until by the year 1690 certain internal develop-

HOUSE, BRIDGELAND STREET, BIDEFORD.
Late seventeenth century, with early nineteenth-century facing of stucco.

ments, including Bridgeland Street, were determined upon and Nathaniel Gascoyne appointed architect and builder. It is conjectured that Gascoyne acted as architect for No. 28 Bridgeland Street (see page 87). This house, built between 1691–93, is evidence of the influence of the vernacular style common to other parts of England. From the ground line to the modillion cornice it would rank as an important house of the Carolean period in any part of the country, but above the cornice its features are of local stamp and earlier mien. The semi-bow window with the quadrant corners was added at the beginning of the nineteenth century when the roof was reslated. The house has a spacious courtyard and an interesting relic of the old Colonial days in the form of a milestone with the legend : " Seven miles from New

York Ferry," which may have found its way into the hold of a trading brig as ballast.

The other house selected for illustration is evidently by the same architect-builder, but it owes its weathercoat of stucco to early nineteenth-century prejudice against the texture of honest brick. As is to be expected from a town wherein the interest was mainly that of shipping and the sea, the joinery of staircases, panelling and door-trims exhibit quips and conceits of unique and humorous shape. Most of the staircases are spacious, with handrails ramped to aid the ascent, with spiral balusters twisted with delicacy and skill, which together with the capped newel posts and odd columns thrown in to support upper flights and landings, form perspectives of ineffable charm, enhanced by the softness of top lighting. While Bideford remained true to her patriotic instincts in the external renderings of her streets at the formative stage of the tradition, she was not averse to patronising the foreigner who could accomplish internal decoration. There are many finely modelled plaster ceilings in the town said to be the work of a group of Italians who came over at the express wish of certain local residents. If this account is true, the secret of the magnificent ceilings at the Kingsley Rooms and within the Royal Hotel is made clear. The crush of fiddles which form the ornate centre of the ceiling in a house at Torrington is typical of the spirit of this group of Italian plaster workers.

HOUSE, SMITH STREET, TORRINGTON. 1702.

Torrington, which is also on the Torridge, holds several houses of the formative period. The house in Smith Street, which dates from 1702, best expresses the definite ordering to which the attributes of sashed windows and wooden cornice and alternating dormer pediments contributed.

By the year 1720 regional architecture of the formative period had become fairly established in the town and about the countryside. The newer learning from divers sources had become part of the vernacular, but it was reserved for the more important houses. With the influence of ideas from London and Bristol and the activities of Sir John Vanbrugh at Plymouth, particularly the building of the Gun Wharf at Plymouth Dock, the first quarter of the eighteenth century saw the western region prepared to accept classic forms as then understood in the neighbourhood of the metropolis. Half a century had passed since the partial destruction of London by fire; in the interim she had responded to the wizardry of Sir Christopher

DEVONPORT DOCKYARD.
House of early eighteenth-century date.

Wren and like a phœnix was new risen from the ashes. London now reasserted her ascendancy, the era of experiments with Dutch and French motifs and ornaments had given place to a definite vernacular which became currency in the remotest parts of England. But the west country had its own method of assimilating the new learning. The old Spartan instinct for breadth and simplicity was too strong to be entirely displaced, the pleasant homely expression of other days was too deep rooted to give way to Hanoverian taste. Hence it was that time-honoured methods of building stone walls, of roofing with thatch and the forming of cottages and farm-houses of cob, long and low in proportion, proceeded side by side with the building of expensive brick and stone houses for those in a position to afford such outlay. That a distinctive style came about at the close of the seventeenth century is a proven fact, and that the seeds thus sown bore fruitful results in the years that followed can be seen from the illustrations and the description of the movement as given in the ensuing sections of this chapter.

CHAPTER V

THE MIDDLE PERIOD (1730–1780)

REGIONAL DISTINCTIONS FURTHER EXPLAINED FROM THE REIGN OF GEORGE THE FIRST TO THE PERIOD OF CLASSICAL REFINEMENT

THE transition from the formative to the next stage in regional building is marked by a series of overlappings, yet the process of evolution is definite, and structure as structure continues articulate. The change was gradual and almost imperceptible, much as the merging of youth into manhood. A fresh current had arisen to direct the social amenities of the eighteenth century which had begun with the Restoration. In the sphere of building

SALTRAM HOUSE, DEVONSHIRE.

the main impetus as far as patronage of the crafts was concerned came from the "middling" sort of people, the squirearchy and the merchants, who in turn had a following among people in less prosperous circumstances. This explains the strength as well as the scope of the vernacular. On the other hand, it is equally true that the building of mansions for the nobility and the landed gentry gave employment to a host of builders, masons, bricklayers, and carpenters as well as to the upholsterers of London, Bath, and Bristol. In the latter case the plans were prepared under the direction of a London architect, who assumed direction of affairs, and the labour as well as the material was supplied by the estate. On this and other counts the

CARCLEW, NEAR TRURO. MAIN FRONT. 1749.
William Edwards, Architect.

CARCLEW, NEAR TRURO. GARDEN FRONT. 1749.
William Edwards, Architect.

weight and substance of the building movement can be assigned to the first-named patronage which collectively sustained the trades.

The purpose of this work, therefore, is to treat of the regional distinctions as a whole rather than to call attention to a specific section of the tradition, as for example, the style and purpose of the west-country mansion. The great houses form a distinct phase by themselves, but they involve considerations of estate development as well as of ancillary buildings and minor attributes.

Among the mansions erected in Devonshire at the close of the seventeenth century and during the first half of the eighteenth the following are representative :

HALDON HOUSE, DEVONSHIRE.

Coryton, 1754 ; Castlehill, the seat of Lord Fortescue which was built in 1760 ; Haldon House in 1750 ; Maristow in 1740 and Ugbrooke in 1730. All these houses are representative of tendencies common to the mansions of contemporary date in other parts of England. They were projected on the great scale with suites of apartments richly decorated, but with the exception of Haldon House, originally the seat of the Palk family, do not exhibit features of outstanding interest. At Haldon the designer attempted an interesting composition in which the mansion forms an imposing central feature recessed between balancing wings after the Palladian mode. Saltram, which is interesting by reason of its scale and the style of its fitments, belongs to the first quarter of the eighteenth century.

Despite the scenic attractions of Devonshire and its popularity as a residential country, it is to Cornwall that attention must be directed for the typical mansion of the middle period. Of those of early date can be cited the small manor at St. Tudy, the ancestral home of the Kekewich family, and Newton Ferrers, near Callington, a plain two-storied house of homely dignity dating from 1705. Antony House, near St. Germans; Modintonham, near Saltash; Carclew, 1744; Tregenna Castle, St. Ives, 1764, as well as many other mansions of lesser importance.

It is convenient to take the year 1718 as the turning-point in the trend of the contemporary regional style in so far as Cornwall is to be regarded. For by this time Sir John Vanbrugh was at work on the Gun Wharf at Plymouth Dock and had

SALTRAM HOUSE, DEVONSHIRE.

prepared his plans and elevations for the Commissioner's house near by, which still exists as a happy instance of his somewhat megalithic treatment. Antony House, which was built three years later for Sir William Carew, owes its inception to the genius of James Gibbs, who prepared the plans for the Cornish masons. It is an exceptionally fine example of Gibbs' matured manner, the exterior as well as the design of the staircase and the richly simple decoration of the apartments rivalling the work of William Kent. It is certain that the influence of Gibbs' diction in the handling of this classic example had an immediate effect on the building style in the vicinity, for in no other way and to no other source can be attributed the finesse of the rectory at Callington, a small granite-built house of ordinary dimensions, but of superlative charm. A few years since the front door of this house was moved to

TOWN HOUSE AT TRURO. 1759.

the south flank of the building, thereby detracting from the finished effect of the main front. Carclew, near Truro, built from the designs of William Edwards, a self-educated architect, shows close reference to the Gibbs' model, as exemplified in the design and style of Antony. The principal front faces south and has an unique arrangement of balancing loggias connecting the main front to the wings. There is no other façade of the size in England which reveals such consummate skill in the grouping of the component masses.

For further evidence of the reception of the classic ideal and the commingling

TOWN HOUSE, TRURO. STAIRCASE AND WALL PANELS. 1759.

TOWN HOUSE, TRURO. DETAIL OF BALUSTRADE TO STAIRCASE. 1759.

of its attributes with native ideas of articulation attention should be given to the houses on the hill at Saltash, where the streets rise from the Tamar, to the fine town houses of the period at Liskeard, Launceston, Bodmin, and Truro. By 1750 the new leavening of precise detail and rhythmic spacing had become common practice among the old architect-builders westward from Plymouth to Penzance. It is evident that the builders of Bath, Bristol, and Exeter assisted the development, but it is also sure as it is logical and true that local conditions materially aided the vernacular expression. As the eighteenth century approached its waning years the interest of the Cornish gentry in building matters, aided by the publication of Borlase's *Antiquities*, showed a taste for castellated architecture in the " good old Cornish manner," but the

H

enthusiasm of the few did little to check the main tide which remained consistent to its original impetus. Restormel House is a case in point. Tregenna Castle, above St. Ives, is a more concrete example of " Gothick " taste, but it remains true to the theory of a formal plan and sashed windows for the openings as well as contemporary classic detail for the fireplaces and joinery. Perhaps the zenith of style was reached in the design of the stone-fronted house at Truro built in the year 1759 as a nobleman's winter residence. The detail in this house, both externally and internally,

TOWN HOUSE, TRURO.   CEILING IN DINING-ROOM.   1759.

is equal to the finest achievements of Isaac Ware and Sir Robert Taylor. The illustrations show the main front with its three storeys and a basement as well as the highly ornate detail of the staircase, which has a balustrade of wrought iron, and the free, yet restrained, design of the modelled plaster enrichments introduced for walls and ceilings. As a contrast to the stone houses of Truro of the middle period reference is made to Palmer House, Torrington, which is a most interesting example of brickwork subordinated to a bold Palladian treatment of pilasters and cornice. The house is one of style and consequence. The order is introduced for the purpose of a diversion, in other words, to give emphasis by a three-part grouping in which the centre first attracts the eye. In order to enhance the sense of predetermined composition the builder introduced the twin piers which stand at the extremity of the railings. The present railings belong to the early nineteenth century.

For the purpose of demonstrating the changes in expression that occurred between the years 1750–80, as well as the use of slate as a material for covering

TOWN HOUSE, TRURO. DETAIL OF CEILING IN SALOON. 1759.

brick and stone walls, some typical and representative examples have been chosen for illustration. The first example is from Bridgeland Street, Bideford; a house refronted about 1750, when the twin bay windows were added, and stuccoed over sixty years later. Here the flavour is Palladian, the style being in accord with that then prevalent at Bristol under Wood, of Bath, and slightly reminiscent of the older houses of 1730 at Bridgewater. It is a broad and representative treatment somewhat quizzical in expression, as though the façade felt a little diffident about breaking in on the two-storied fronts of the previous century. Another house of the same date

HOUSE IN BRIDGELAND STREET, BIDEFORD.
1750 Period. Stucco later.

THE CASTLE, EXETER. 1773.

HOUSE IN BRIDGELAND STREET, BIDEFORD. 1750.
Stucco added in 1810.

PALMER HOUSE, TORRINGTON. 1752.

H *

from Bridgeland Street shows a peculiarity in the finish of the heads to the bay, which resemble the head-gear of the time. It is from such whimsicalities that the flavour of the period can be adduced. The three-storied brick house at Topsham is chiefly remarkable for the position of the square bay which runs through three floors. This house belongs to the 1775 period and is a fine example of late brickwork. The white-painted window frames are not flush with the external face of the walling, but have been set within the $4\frac{1}{2}$-in. reveals, but at the same time the marginal surface is retained, affording proof of the partial acceptance of the theory that came into force in London in 1730 regarding the protection of woodwork from fire. The Castle at Exeter (see page 100) was built in 1773, and is evidence of acquaintance with the masonry of Bath and Bristol of Woods' times. In the case of the Customs Watch House on the Barbican at Plymouth, the revival of slate hanging or shingling is encountered. This building has the character of its purpose, there is no mistaking its function, to some extent it is reminiscent of the elegant contemporary Georgian style in America ; from the detail can be gleaned the fact that it was built about the year 1765. The geometrical sashing to the first-floor windows gives a play of line and affords contrast to the widely spaced colonnade below. Of the same date is Millbay House, Plymouth, a building of three stories, stone built and slate hung. In this work local stone is used for the walling, the modillion cornice is of wood and the chimney-stacks are of brick. The silvery effect of the vertical slating and the admirable disposition of the

CUSTOMS WATCH HOUSE, BARBICAN,
PLYMOUTH. 1765.

windows is most telling. This house originally stood in open country, with a fair view of the Cornish hills ; it is typical of west-country methods of the late middle period.

Durnford Street, Stonehouse, and Emma Place belong to the period of 1775. Here is to be seen how the west-country builders dealt with the problem of terrace houses. Durnford Street was at one time a fashionable residential centre for the families of naval officers. The houses are small, but are distinguished by fair proportion and the elegance of the doorways and iron and wood railings to the front areas. About a century since the fronts were stuccoed to accord with the theories of Foulston. Emma Place, Stonehouse, shows in its grouping an advance on the houses in Durnford Street, the pedimented features to the end houses following the character of the administrative block at the Naval Hospital. For variety of interest and picturesque grouping attention is directed to the back elevation of the Durnford Street houses on the west side. Here can be seen bow and bay windows, tall dormers and spy places ranged in order like the stern quarters of three deckers and frigates. The backs are slate hung, and although in bad repair and encumbered with excrescences have an interest which is unique.

Perhaps the finest specimen of the 1775 period is Nelson House, St. Aubyn

MILLBAY HOUSE, PLYMOUTH. 1765.
Back elevation showing vertical slating and modillion cornice of wood. Chimney stacks of brick.

Street, Devonport, the front of which is without compeer for unaffected grace; by this time the Adam mode had become common in Plymouth and flourished side by side with brick fronts which inherited features of earlier and broader dialect. In this house it is the silver-tongued Devonian who speaks, one who has had acquaintance with the polish of Bath. The architect-builder, without knowing it, had stumbled upon a species of baroque design as a protest against the flat fronts of other towns. The bow windows are spacious and well conceived, the contrast of horizontal and vertical sub-divisionings is excellent, and the species of dome over

DURNFORD STREET, STONEHOUSE. TERRACE HOUSES. 1775.

EMMA PLACE, STONEHOUSE. 1775.

the porch and the flutings of the cornice frame in the horizontal striations of the slate hanging. It is a pleasant and humane house with a personality, the sort of house an author would select as a scene for romantic action. Yet the original builder had no other purpose in view but to provide a home for a worthy townsman, which would be strong, commodious and fair to look upon.

As previously pointed out, by the year 1775 the refinement of style made possible by the perfect craftsmanship in stone, wood, and stucco on the part of the craftsman who, in districts near to London, took their cue from Sir Robert Taylor and the Adams brothers, had passed with lightning rapidity to the west country. Progress was no longer slow, but notwithstanding improved transport, the publication of books, and the promulgation of precise instructions for the use of all and sundry, the west-country workers accepted the latest

Nos. 85 AND 86 DURNFORD STREET, STONEHOUSE. 1775.
Note linking of doorways.

NELSON HOUSE, ST. AUBYN STREET, DEVONPORT. 1775.

theories at face value only and proceeded forthwith to recast metropolitan ideas to suit their own theories of the way things should be done. The building of Whiteford House, near Stoke Climsland, in 1775 is the tidal mark reached by regional architecture of the late middle period. The house was projected by Sir William Call, a retired nabob, who obtained plans from London and proceeded to build for himself. The house was pulled down in 1913. Local artisans worked Kit Hill granite for the walls and shaped the massive granite cornice. Local carpenters formed the mahogany-sashed windows and Walter Storey Wivel took a pride in designing the mahogany staircase, one of the finest in England.

DURNFORD STREET, STONEHOUSE. 1775. BACKS OF HOUSES.

WHITEFORD, STOKE CLIMSLAND, CORNWALL. THE TEMPLE.
Now used as a cattle byre. The three arched openings were originally sashed.

Determined that his work should be remembered, Master Wivel pencilled his name and the date of completion on one of the fir carriages out of sight. Sir William Call built Whiteford regardless of expense ; he engaged Italians from London to model the ornate plaster ceilings to the principal rooms and to fashion the vaulted corridors and lobbies. The stable buildings accorded with the state of the house. The garden house, of which an illustration is given—it is now a cattle byre—was devised of cut granite with ornamental panels from Mrs. Coade's factory at Lambeth. It is evident that the nabob wished to possess a palace. Some of the marble fireplaces and a portion of the balustrade were removed to Mount Edgcumbe thirty years since. The rest of the material, including most of the worked granite, has been reused in the new Manor Farm-house, which is the property of His Royal Highness the Prince of Wales.

From this summarised discussion of the salient features of the middle period certain deductions can be made. It has, however, been thought expedient to recount the inevitable overlappings which the regional building evolution shows partly in the descriptions of Exeter and Plymouth, wholly in the introductory chapter and again in the conclusion. The main point to be considered is that from whatever source the inspiration came, no matter at what time, or under any specific pressure or impetus, before it passed into the currency of Devon or Cornwall it was first subjected to the assay standard of regional taste.

CHAPTER VI

THE LATE PERIOD (1780–1810)

WHICH TREATS OF STYLISTIC REFINEMENT AND PRECISION IN MINOR AFFAIRS AS WELL AS ECONOMY IN THE USE OF MATERIALS

AS is to be expected, buildings of all types erected during the late period in the West of England show more regard for structural economy than those of the preceding years. It is not unusual to find brick-built houses in stone districts, not only in towns but in the heart of the country ; the detail, however, exhibits greater refinement, and while conforming to standard yet admits of considerable license in execution. By this time definite links had been forged and the chain of sequence was in operation. The main centres, such as Exeter and Plymouth, as far as social amenities are concerned, responded directly to the heart-beats of the capital, as well as to impulses from Bath and Bristol ; but the builders and craftsmen had their own point of view and could not, even if they had desired it, escape from the time-honoured renderings to which their communal instincts tended. Building was still an affair of structure, but it had caught the stylistic flavour of the time even in its humbler aspirations. Door-trims, hood and pentice, crowning, cornice, plat-band and dormer finish, lead rainwater head, and sashed window, as well as other details, show the desire of the local builders, as well as reflecting the opinions of those for whom the houses were built, to be thought as polite and genteel as the people of London town. At this time London influence was in the ascendant, especially so in the case of the town houses and public buildings of Exeter, Plymouth, and Truro ; but the cottages and farm-houses, while exhibiting slight changes of detail in the parts produced by the skill of carpenters, in the main fabric carry traditional and fundamental associations of broad walling surface and small windows ; of roofs formed of small slates or close thatching and with chimney-stacks of direct form and stepping which are a delight to behold. At Looe, Polperro, Fowey, Falmouth, and St. Ives can be seen some of the most fascinating examples of cottages and small houses, the work of local builders of the late period, in which the attributes are almost wholly regional. For example, the console brackets to the projecting door-heads and pentices, while carrying a simple version of classic mouldings, are shaped in fantastic fashion and show in a remarkable way the sea-

HOUSE AT TOPSHAM, DEVON. 1708.

108

MOUNT WISE, DEVONPORT.
Group of small houses, showing slate hanging.

DOUBLE HOUSE, TAVISTOCK, DEVON. 1802.
Showing slate hanging.

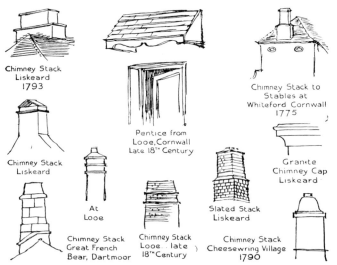

Chimney Stack
Liskeard
1793

Chimney Stack
Liskeard

At
Looe

Chimney Stack
Great French
Bear, Dartmoor

Pentice from
Looe, Cornwall
Late 18ᵀᴴ Century

Chimney Stack
Looe. late
18ᵀᴴ Century

Slated Stack
Liskeard

Chimney Stack
Cheesewring Village
1790

Chimney Stack to
Stables at
Whiteford Cornwall
1775

Granite
Chimney Cap
Liskeard

faring occupations of the locality. In such places as those mentioned, as well as for farm-houses and cottages in the vicinity, it is still customary to colour the external walls with a lime wash which varies from ochre to lemon, green, pink, and orange, proof of the survival of mediæval practice as well as knowledge of similar methods peculiar to Brittany and the coastal villages of France. From 1780 onwards slate hanging for external walling enters upon its ultimate phase; this is particularly the case in Cornwall, where its use was continued until John Foulston initiated his scheme of stucco dressing over rough stone and brick. Prince Hall on Dartmoor, which was built in 1785, is a noteworthy example of slate hanging. Slate was employed in this way as a precautionary measure against damp and driving rain. Under the old custom vertical battens were first fixed to the walls and then carried with horizontal slating battens to which the slates are attached, breaking bond as in the case of roof slating and showing a neat margin, the result being a species of hollow wall which has the merit of being extremely rich in texture and affording a fine contrast of colour with the neatly

COTTAGE AT LOOE, CORNWALL.
1780.

sashed windows and the white paint of the main cornice and trims. Sometimes the slate is used to encase the chimney-stacks and the gable ends. Another picturesque example of slightly later date is the "Plume of Feathers," the oldest building in Princetown; mention has already been made of the backs of the houses on the west side of Durnford Street, Stonehouse. The builders of the late phase in the western region were

Brickwork →

Section

Detail of Wooden Cornice
George Street, Plymouth
1795

Early Nineteenth Century
Cornice. Liskeard

Cornice to –
Group of Cottages,
Smithwick Street,
Falmouth 1780

Wood Cornice.
Durnford Street,
Stonehouse
1780

Slate Hanging

HOUSE, HIGH STREET, BIDEFORD.
Early nineteenth century.

THE INN, COUNTESS WEIR, DEVON. 1815.

THE POST OFFICE, KENTON, DEVON. 1817.

THE RETREAT, NEAR TOPSHAM, EXETER. LODGES AT ENTRANCE GATE. 1790.

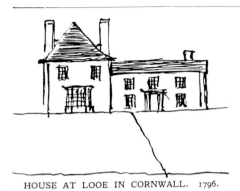

HOUSE AT LOOE IN CORNWALL. 1796.

CHIMNEY STACK.
CAPPING IN GRANITE.
1805.

FARM-HOUSE, CARDENHAM MOOR,
CORNWALL. 1795.

honest adherents to the earliest form of building known; without profound knowledge of historical precedent they, by experiment, arrived at the first principles of building followed in Homeric times. They knew how to use large stones for walls, when to introduce bond timbers of suitable scantling, and where to give accent to salient points by worked membering. Slate scripping also came in handy to protect the exposed ends of main constructional timbers. The opposition of such regional practice to the newer leavening of stylistic detail, which reached the west country in a never-ceasing stream, produced the definite tradition now discussed which is at once the despair and the admiration of the modern architect. At Baker's Place, Stonehouse, will be seen a small range of cottages two storeys high, of the date 1806, which at one time were the homes of slaters and carpenters. On the wall of one of

BAKERS PLACE,
1806
PHILLIPS PATENT METHOD
OF SLATING AND TILING BELOW
IS HIS EVERLASTING COATING
OR PATENT WEATHER AND FIREPROOF
COMPOSITION

the cottages is the attached legend which, together with a specimen of trellis slating, is accurate and telling evidence of the craftsmanship of the day.

From 1780 onwards many minor improvements were introduced into domestic building, including larger windows, projecting balconies of iron and wood, and in the sphere of planning we find geometrical rooms, including those circular, elliptical and octagonal in shape. The treatment of the 1790 addition to the " Courtenay Arms " at Starcross, near Dawlish, is typical of the desire to secure a sea prospect (see page 115).

At Mount Wise there is a group of small " genteel " houses which form an unique retired settlement. The approach is from

GATE PIER
TERMINAL,
EMMA PLACE,
STONEHOUSE.
1780.

MARKET HOUSE, LOSTWITHIEL.
Erected by Lord Mount Edgcumbe, 1781.

DOUBLE DOOR AT TRURO. 1806.

I

TOR ROYAL, DARTMOOR, DEVON. 1795–1820.
The property of His Royal Highness the Prince of Wales. The gambrel roof to the centre building was added in 1912.

a private drive. There is a small harbour with bathing place and the wharf is embellished with shrubs. Here the charm of silvery slate hanging, white paint and delicate detail is seen at its best, the ensemble belongs entirely to the west country. The buildings in their grouping are neither formal nor haphazard, on the contrary, they show definitive planning suited to the site. The date of these houses is about 1795 (see page 109). One of the most satisfactory examples of slate hanging occurs at Tavistock. Built in 1802, this double house is evidence of the group of simple lines so essential to direct statement. The slate hanging in this case is carried in horizontal lines across the arcuations of the doors and the bays forming the central features. John Foulston, whose work properly belongs to the next phase, also had recourse to slate hanging as a finish to his stucco fronts. At the end of St. Michael's Terrace (see page 116) the judicious ramping of the walls to suit the several heights and the use of slating has resulted in a very finished effect, other characteristics of the late period including such features as wooden cornices of diminutive scale and delicate membering. There are the pear-drop cornices of George Street, Plymouth, to set off the plain brickwork of the walling below, and Devonport also can show similar domestic examples of remarkable delicacy.

Reverting to the subject of bow windows the attention of the reader is directed to the several fine examples in High Street, Exeter, some

THE COURTENAY ARMS, DEVON. BOW WINDOW AND BALCONY.
Late eighteenth century.

of which (as the illustrations show) extend through three storeys. In this case stucco forms the basis of the external design, which does not aim at deception as to the nature of the material; on the contrary, it is evident that the designer aimed at neatness and precision and sought rather to impart a sense of cohesion to the work by employing the horizontal and vertical lines of the surface to contrast with the three-light windows of each storey through which the segmental bow passes. Another example of the bow window with rusticated stucco for the finish of the walling is to be seen at Bideford, about 1802 (see page 111), while the post office at Kenton, built about 1810, is a good specimen of the treatment of flat segmental bows to a house of small size. The inn at Countess Weir, built about the same time, is chiefly remarkable for the repetition of the three light Wyatt windows.

A representative example of the small country house of the period is Tor Royal, on Dartmoor, the property of His Royal Highness the Prince of Wales. Built in 1795 as a country residence for Sir Thomas Tyrwhitt, its plan originally followed the usual arrangement of a central hall with a staircase and rooms on the right and left, the kitchen and offices being in a wing to the left of the entrance. At a later

ST. MICHAEL'S TERRACE, STOKE DAMAREL (End house, showing slate hanging).
John Foulston, Architect.

date an additional suite of rooms was added. The illustration on page 114 shows the house as it appears to-day. The roof has been remodelled, but otherwise the building is much as it was a century ago when Sir Thomas Tyrwhitt had included the fitments he had recently secured from Carleton House, London, which Holland designed. Tor Royal not only shows a minor aspect of building on Dartmoor according to local theories, but in the character of the courtyard features, such as the tower with its octagonal turret and the entrance lodge (see pages 117 and 120), reflects the striking economy of style combined with good taste essential alike to the requirements of the owner and the locality.

TOR ROYAL, PRINCETOWN, DEVON. TOWER AND TURRET IN COURTYARD. 1795-1796.

1 *

A very finished " Lodge " composition is that formed by the twin lodges and gates to the " Retreat," near Topsham, Exeter, mentioned by Joseph Farington ; here the keynote is one of rich simplicity. It must not be thought that contemporary builders neglected to employ dressed stone and granite for small houses whatever the attractions of slate and stucco. There is, for example, the diminutive Market House at Camelford, the stone houses at Truro and the three-part group forming a portion of the building group at the Naval Hospital, Stonehouse (see illustrations).

The Market House at Camelford belongs to the 1790 period, and to the same

BOW-FRONTED HOUSE. HIGH STREET,
EXETER. 1805.
Stucco contemporary.

date can be ascribed the satisfactory house at the eastern extremity of the town, which has the original palisade in the Chinese taste.

Lady Drake's House at Lympstone, which was built in 1810 (see page 119), has all the attributes of the contemporary Empire style as exemplified in Krafft's illustrations of French villas. It is four storeys high at the centre, including the basement storey and the attics. The composition belongs to the succeeding phase which Foulston and his successors made popular, but the detail corresponds more exactly to the Adamesque manner. It is a demure house, approaching a mansion in size and, from a distance, looks larger than it really is. If an example illustrating early nineteenth-century taste, typical of the people Jane Austen portrays, this house assuredly fits the case. The more the subject of regional building in the West of England is subjected to enquiry the more apparent becomes the rich diversity of forms and type peculiar to every district of Devon and Cornwall. The wonder is that without out a definite school or a directing coterie of architects the convincing result could have been attained. It is true that builders in the late period were backed by the authentic models of London, Bath, and Bristol, but it is equally true that their own inherent sense of fitness as well as observance of traditional methods of construction and the employment of local materials helped them in their decisions. The architecture of the western region never lacks the stamp of locale ; the old houses seem at one with the scenery, they are never forced in gesture, yet all and sundry have scale and individuality and, although in a sense the external arrangements are standardised, no two houses can be said to be alike. The secret of the style lies in the simplicity of the silhouette, for no matter whether the house be the simple type such as the one on the edge of Cardenham Moor or the Jamaica Inn on Bodmin Moor, regularity of subordinate features is always

LADY DRAKE'S HOUSE, LYMPSTONE, EXETER. DEVON. 1810.

HOUSE AT CAMELFORD, CORNWALL. 1790.

adjusted to some slight asymmetrical distinction arising out of the requirements of structure, which is complete and satisfying to the eye.

At Falmouth the student of such matters will be confronted with some noteworthy specimens, particularly of detail of the late period. There are the ornamental fanlights to the doorways of the houses, the wooden shop-fronts sashed according to draft. There is the Royal Hotel replete with its geometrical staircase and wrought-iron balustrade, with the coach office below. Falmouth, too, can show fine compo-

TOR ROYAL, PRINCETOWN, DEVON. ENTRANCE LODGE. 1795.

sitions of several houses in a row, such as the group in Arwenack Road, now the Sailor's Home, and the town houses with the important bay window of three storeys, now the Spanish Consulate. The old importance of the place when the smart packets sailed from the bay to America has vanished, but the buildings remain to show former state and prosperity. As one journeys along the western roads to Truro, Redruth, Camborne, St. Ives, and Penzance the influence of the late period becomes increasingly insistent, but it is a style always tempered with humane if simple touches, suggesting that the builders were inspired to rise above the petty

STONE HOUSES, TRURO.   1802.

STONE HOUSES, TRURO. 1805.

dictates of fashion and to express themselves directly; in no other way can the personal touches be described.

Penzance is not without its charm, but it is a dull town by comparison with Falmouth. At St. Ives, on the other hand, regional building is seen as its best, and for this reason a short description of the town is given.

The best view of old St. Ives is that gained from above, when the houses appear in clustering groups, with the harbour on the south side of the Island and Admiralty

THREE HOUSES, NAVAL HOSPITAL, STONEHOUSE. 1800.

Station. In the midst arising above the grey assemblage is the ancient church of St. Nicholas standing like a friar amidst a group of followers. The houses crowd promiscuously side by side and follow the contours as though every inch of ground is too precious to lose. Shelter is thus obtained from the northern gales; the ways between the houses are narrow, while the weather coats of silver-grey slating are eloquent of hard weather and simple faring. Yet, notwithstanding the close building, there is a sense of sea pride and tidiness in the white paint, the brass door-knockers and latches. The houses can be likened to the womenfolk such are their feminine characteristics, and the fishing fleet can stand for the masculine side of the town's

COTTAGE, BUNKER'S HILL, ST. IVES, CORNWALL. 1810.

life. St. Ives compels affection; even the casual visitor comes immediately under its spell. The streets have to be traversed separately before local topography can be grasped, for the fishing port is a modest retiring place. There are numerous ways and dive holes between the houses down to the harbour, through which the spray of the Atlantic can be glimpsed, vistas of incomparable charm punctuated with the needle masts and the black hulls of craft that have weathered many a gale. Half-way along the harbour wall can be seen the squat lighthouse devised by Smeaton, standing as a benevolent sentinel, somewhat jealous it seems of the toy light shaft and revolving lantern at the end of the pier. St. Ives is the product of two centuries of granite shaping, but the town is proud of such brick houses as the "Retreat," which show how the rulings of the Georges were observed even in lawless times. The

COTTAGE IN ADMIRAL'S HARD, STONEHOUSE. 1809.

GROUP OF FARM BUILDINGS NEAR CALLINGTON, CORNWALL. 1793.

brickwork appears amidst the grey stone much as red-coated Hanoverian soldiers would have cut a fine dash amidst the fishermen, pipe-clayed facings, tall cap and all.

It is evident, too, that the old builders were not averse to following the different influences that came westwards; for example, there is evidence in the small wood cornices, the fanlights, the door-knocker and the wrought-iron railings. In almost every case the fisherman's home proper begins at the top of a granite flight of steps; the basement being reserved for curing and packing fish and perhaps in other days served to store kegs of rum and brandy. Like Polperro, St. Ives is an artist's town; old cottages have been converted into studios, and casement cloth for window curtains now replaces the dimity of the eighteenth century which came down in bales by sea from Bristol.

It is of interest to note that many of the granite houses belong to the period 1780-1810. The majority were built by one James Shrugg, builder and stonemason, of St. Ives, whom, we learn, had issue and many descendants who eventually carried the secrets of regional building to Australia.

GRANITE-BUILT COTTAGES, ST. IVES, CORNWALL.

The late period is important on two counts, first because it reveals the continuance of the earlier phases of style and settled method of working local materials, and secondly because it favoured standardised and precise detail. In the case of St. Ives and Penzance the newer information can be traced to Bristol, to which place the direct way was by sea. It is evident, however, that apart from the comparative remoteness of Devon and Cornwall from the metropolis the building activities of London architects did eventually reach out-of-the-way parts, and this fact accounts for regional architecture in the west retaining its vivacity until the middle of the Victorian era. At this juncture the description of regional building must turn to the work that succeeded to the impulses of the eighteenth century. There is, however, no definite division between the phases other than the limitation imposed by the dates, which are purely arbitrary, the inevitable overlappings of style and fashion serving to throw into stronger relief the continuity of the development as a whole.

CHAPTER VII

REGENCY AND EARLY VICTORIAN (1810–1850)

IN WHICH IS GIVEN A DESCRIPTION OF THE LATEST PHASES OF THE TRADITION
AND AN ACCOUNT OF ITS SURVIVAL AS A MEANS OF REGIONAL EXPRESSION UNTIL
THE MIDDLE OF THE NINETEENTH CENTURY

IT is an attribute of architecture to record the temperament of an age, to mark incidental changes of taste, as one generation gives place to another, and to hint at the attitude of those responsible for the work in being. The foregoing, with other qualities which have been mentioned in these pages, goes

PENRYN, CORNWALL.
A town with many Regency characteristics.

far to explain the appeal right building makes to seeing eyes. To the generality of people architecture is an esoteric if a concrete fact. It is accepted without question as something inevitable, and becomes familiar as conventional scenery; there enquiry ends, but, paradoxical as it may appear, buildings of unorthodox stamp and brutal expression, and there are many such, are the first to be acclaimed. This apathy on the part of the general public is now in a fair way to be removed; it arose,

HOUSE AT DAWLISH, DEVON. 1817 (At one time the home of Sir John Rennie).
John Nash, Architect.

STONELANDS, DAWLISH. THE HALL. 1817.
John Nash, Architect.

FREMINGTON, NORTH DEVON. 1820.

HOUSE AT TOPSHAM, DEVON. SHOWING STUCCO ADDITIONS OF 1825.

in the first place, when traditional usage declined, a natural consequence due to the diverting of industry into channels entirely opposed to limited production. The change began with the close of the eighteenth-century, but the impetus of the age of good taste was too powerful to submit instanter to forces which it

A HOUSE AT TRURO. 1805.

instinctively distrusted ; as a result the eighteenth century spirit which had its beginnings with the Restoration continued in most parts of England until the accession of Queen Victoria ; in the west country it was continued in some districts until the

WROUGHT-IRON BRACKETS
TO DOOR-HOOD,
LOSTWITHIEL. 1812.

ADELAIDE PLACE, STONEHOUSE. 1820.
John Foulston, Architect.

COMPOSITION, NEAR CAMBORNE, CORNWALL.
Early nineteenth century.

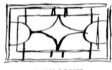

FANLIGHT,
LOSTWITHIEL. 1815.

year of the Great Exhibition. Regional architecture, therefore, in the early nineteenth century can be said to have remained constant to its original acceptance of the classic view-point. It is equally true that the western style as a whole, for as a distinct if closely related branch of the national style it must be considered, was at one with

THE CUSTOMS HOUSE, LOOE. 1812.

the temper of the people ; prior to the year 1800 vernacular building was in harmony with the houses of the nobility, or, to be precise, in so far as externals are to be considered. From the standpoint of domestic expression it was a neat style and one conscious of its breeding, proud, too, in a modest way, of its tidiness. From 1790 to 1810 the classic influence was at its zenith, a result due to the experience of over a century;

K

during these twenty years building expression had reached a point when its tone was sufficiently strong to react on the minor arts and crafts ; and to the congenial and intimate nature of the domestic branch of building was added the individuality revealed in the detail, which attribute, despite the standardisation of the main features, accounts for all that is best in the shaping of the furniture and household appointments. It was an age of studied expression and formality, one of attitude, gesture, and deportment, a time of ceremony and etiquette when class distinctions were rigidly kept. Culture as then understood was the prerogative of the educated ; yet such was the influence of pomp and ceremony that democracy in its ascending stages, unsullied by intensive industrialism, aimed at an observance of gentility which found an outlet in building of houses and the making of furniture. It is equally true, whether the English tradition of the time is considered as a whole or by regional sections, that the Golden Age from 1790 to 1810 represents the tidal mark of the national respect for the arts and crafts which had its beginning in the Middle Ages, and eventually by assimilating foreign ideas came to be not the least important branch of the Renaissance. The spirit of the age was one of restraint, the artistic ideal was high ; forced back on her own resources by events on the Continent, England continued to express her insularity by intensive study of the antique, but what her artists borrowed from Greece and Rome they made their own.

SEVEN STARS HOTEL, TOTNES. 1825.

Perhaps the most remarkable circumstances of the time is the introduction of sculptural modelling by such a master as Flaxman for the decoration of Wedgwood pottery, so prized then as now. Then, too, must be considered the mezzotint engravings after Morland and Wheatley, the aquatints by Malton, the awakened interest in British Archæology and the establishment of the circulating library. The very concentration of artistic interest in itself foreshadowed the great changes of the nineteenth century. From the north came the rhythmical beat of the beam engine, which was soon to leave its bed and move about the land as on the face of the waters ; the century of home life and content was to be succeeded by a period

HOUSE AT LISKEARD, CORNWALL. 1820.

of feverish activity, foreign in every way to the soothing glamour of feudal twilight and the comfort of homely hearths. The long struggle with France came to an end with Waterloo, and the inevitable reaction in home affairs, with the accompanying political battles which aimed at consolidation and reform, ensued. English goods at this period were of the first importance to Continental and American markets, both as regards quality and mass production, and in response to commercial enterprise as well as to the development of steam power a vast industrial population

GROUP OF STUCCO HOUSES, TRURO. 1825.
Late Regency.

sprang into being. Small wonder then that as a result of the domestic and internal changes a species of Babylonian confusion followed in so far as building was concerned, and in the other arts a corresponding disturbance set in. It was at the beginning an age of eclecticism in which respect was paid to any known style ; it produced alike the dreamers of the Romantic school and the stalwart architect-engineers skilled in the use of iron. The outcome of such rivalry between the opposing factions both aiming at intellectual superiority in turn brought about the inevitable battle of the styles. The builders of the western region in the midst of the turmoil remained constant to local custom, and to this factor is due the fine observance of structure leavened with a knowledgeable handling of classic detail which is apparent in the later buildings of the first half of the nineteenth century in Devon and Cornwall.

From 1810 until 1830 the style of building is of a severe classic type; it includes the so-called "Regency" which Nash and his contemporaries deemed suitable for London improvements, as well as a close application of Greek detail, especially of the Doric order, obtained from Stuart and Revett's book, which had appeared half a century previously. It was the time for "Grecian gusto" as distinct from the finesse of the Roman Palladian and Græco-Roman of the late eighteenth-century architects; the delicate modelling of the aquatint was yielding to lithography. Winslade Lodge, at Clyst St. Mary, built in 1812, is an instance of an entrance lodge conceived, as

THE ROYAL HOTEL, HORSEBRIDGE, CORNWALL. 1820.

was fondly thought, in the best style of Athenian grace. Another example of Regency taste is "Stonelands," Dawlish, dating from the year 1817; it is a fair-sized villa from the pencil of John Nash, and is of interest for the fact that it became the home of Sir John Rennie, the architect-engineer whose works have already been mentioned. "Stonelands" is an example of architect's architecture, as was to be expected from a man like John Nash, but even this master of scenic effects came under the spell of Devonshire and his work subconsciously expressed the local building dialect. The houses of this period are invariably finished with stucco. There are examples of stucco channelling, in imitation of stone rustication as well as plain surfaces, at Starcross in Devon and at Truro in Cornwall, as well as the terrace groups of Plymouth, Torquay, and Penzance; to this period can be assigned the practice of applying a stucco skin to early houses of the previous century, as at Exeter and Topsham (see page 128).

One of the most interesting of the small houses of 1820 date, after the Stonelands model, is the Rectory at Fremington, North Devon (see page 128). And the bow-fronted houses in Bridgeland Street, Bideford, are also representative of the change of style. The aspect of a west-country town replete with the habiliments of the Regency is best judged from the present view of Penryn in Cornwall. In the country, however, the older traditions were continued, particularly as regards form and composition. At the Pentilly estate office, built in 1820, the central building is of

K *

TRELLISICK HOUSE, NEAR TRURO, CORNWALL,
William Robinson, Architect,

late eighteenth-century character. There is the storm porch of 1795, which is a feature of Tor Royal on Dartmoor ; the spread of the eaves and the pitch of the roof both follow local custom. The verandah and balcony, on the other hand, is a Regency innovation, and the treatment of the balancing wings and the link walls a throw-back to earlier Palladian models. Strange and incongruous as some of the Gothicised details appear in juxtaposition to classic detail, they are nevertheless quite logical and reflect the close following influence of the Romantic school (see illustration of Pentillie estate office, page 165). Of the Regency hotels, following the building

HOUSE AT STARCROSS, DAWLISH, DEVON.
Early nineteenth century.

of the " Royal " at Plymouth, the " Royal " at Devonport, and Webb's Hotel at Liskeard, the " Seven Stars " at Totnes is one of the most striking instances of architectural skill. The adjustment of the enormous projecting super-porch to the plain wall surface of the building is at once masterly and convincing. Here is evidenced the outlook of the day on the moving world, the anticipation of forces to come, and the welcome to be given.

Of the larger houses of the Regency, Trellisick in Cornwall, built by William Robinson, a pupil of Henry Holland, is representative of the highly Ionic fashion which fast succeeded to the megalithic Doric which Nash and Wilkins both approved for country houses. Robinson in this design followed the teachings of Holland,

HOUSE AT BIDEFORD, DEVON. 1820.

WINSLADE LODGE, CLYST ST. MARY, DEVON. 1815.
Regency Period.

and took as a motif the façade of the old East India House in Leadenhall Street. Trellisick, notwithstanding its monumental portico, is a homely mansion, the south front being not inappropriate to the country and the site. At Liskeard in Cornwall there are several excellent houses of the later period. The one selected for illustration belongs to the period of 1820; it is built of shillet stone and has a range of five sashed windows in two tiers with a recessed porch at the centre. This house demonstrates in a loquacious way the breadth of treatment and logical disposition of features to meet the case, qualities never absent from the houses of the west country, whether they stand as terraces in towns, isolated in the valleys, or at the side of uplands in the country.

At the accession of Queen Victoria a quasi-Italian style was in vogue side by side with a " Gothic " rendering which had nothing in common with the spirit of mediæval custom. But the planning was continued on straightforward lines, room was found for the geometrical staircase with the mahogany handrail, the rooms remained spacious and symmetry was a ruling passion among architects and their following. On the civic side such buildings as the Market House at Penzance, which was won in competition by William Harris, of Bristol, and completed in 1836, and the Market House at Truro stand for the classic aspect of the matured style.

At Redruth there are one or two small works of considerable merit. The granite-fronted house selected for illustration, despite the provincial handling of its minor feature at the centre, is an outstanding example of precise masonry. This building was finished in the year 1851, by which time the weathercock of building taste was turning from hour to hour at the mercy of every cross current.

The variety of the style both in detail and grouping has been the theme of the preceding chapters; the wonder is that sustained tradition in the western region lasted longer than in any other part of England. It is not that the building style is totally different from the vernacular of other English counties, or that it is of superior value. Its intrinsical merit lies in its reception of influences from other parts, as well as its strength to absorb matter foreign to its locality and to gain vivacity in the process; this is the distinctive trait of buildings, both great and small. It is, moreover, a plain and direct style, one relying less upon ornament for its effect than upon the necessities of structure and the sterling qualities of local material. In this particular the buildings reflect the spirit of Devon and Cornwall.

COTTAGES AT LUCKETT, NEAR
CALLINGTON. 1820.

CHAPTER VIII

PRINCETOWN ON DARTMOOR

AN ACCOUNT OF THE TOWN AND THE PRINCIPAL BUILDINGS

IT is one of the curiosities of life that current events do not carry the significance of those that have become historical through the passage of time. This aphorism is especially true of towns, and justifies the theory that the historian of a century hence will take up a pen to record the facts attending the growth of what we of the present day term " garden cities," the product of twentieth-century wishes, to enjoy a species of country life. Perhaps it is because the material is newly made, and the facts of social conditions at Hampstead, Letchworth or Welwyn are so well known, that the need of rescuing the story of towns new a century since appears more pressing. It may be that the past makes a stronger appeal by reason of the contrasts presented, but whatever the reason, desire or excuse, there is an opportunity to make a statement.

Princetown is new as towns go ; it stands within the shelter of the Devon Tors fourteen hundred feet above high tide in Plymouth Sound and, no matter what is urged to the contrary, it is a place with an interest entirely and peculiarly its own. Projected in the opening decade of the last century it attained to centennial status the year war broke out. Its history therefore bridges the most interesting period of national life and includes two of the greatest struggles in which this country has been engaged. Princetown was named to honour Prince Florizel. It owed its inception to an English gentleman who was no slight figure in the Carlton House circle, and its realisation to the genius of an architect famed as a constructor. The effect of this assemblage of plain buildings on the minds of visitors is a matter for speculation ; the guide books, as usual, are mute. Our American cousins make pilgrimage to the walled enclosure where their forebears who were prisoners of war pined for the liberty of the States. To our French friends it is a place of evil associations and on that account is left alone. There are excursionists from the neighbouring watering-places who trip by char-à-banc eager to satisfy their eyes regarding the rigours of the penal system, there are the more genuine visitors to whom the aloofness of the place and the expanse of moorland makes a more direct appeal. Lastly, there are the local inhabitants, true to the idiosyncrasies of Dartmoor, who love the moody, broody atmosphere and who appreciate the slate-capped roofs as much as the austerity of local tradition in building. But to the casual observer the place appears dull, it is said to lack that interest which in more populous centres turns night into day. Small wonder then that some show their contempt by flaunting gay paper streamers from moving cars and vent their displeasure accompanied by the strident notes of cornets and accordions.

Here is a town of some importance where one does not expect more than a hamlet of grey cottages a town, moreover, of comparatively recent growth, the same age as the original walls of the prison, with houses of the plainest fronting the four crossways. Princetown has the unique distinction of being the earliest of early nineteenth-century towns. It had a railroad of its own soon after the completion of the coachroad from Exeter to Tavistock, twenty years before Londoners flocked to Euston to see the triumph of Stephenson within their gates. It also boasted

138

DARTMOOR PRISON AND BARRACKS. 1809–1815 (From a contemporary drawing).
Daniel Alexander, Architect.

the largest war prison in the country, larger than the one at Chatham and braver than the pen at Norman Cross, an improvement on the hulks on the Tamar and the Medway, but terrible enough to Napoleon's veterans and conscripts who fought in the Peninsula and in the last scene of the drama.

For such reasons as the foregoing, and they are cogent ones, the town can be wrote up as having played its part in announcing the expansion of modern events under the rule of the monarchs who succeeded George the Third.

Towns, like Topsy, happen and grow, some have the presence of a monastic establishment or a cathedral to which they attribute parentage : Plymouth from a fishing hamlet has become a naval centre. London from being the port of Verulamium has become the capital of the Empire.

Princetown is the most unexpected of places. There are few intricacies of formation, all its secrets are bare to the eye. It revels in its upstart character. A forcibility of statement calculated to take away the breath, a monotony of colour permeating wall and roof, a stiffness of startling severity calling forth feelings of defiance and contempt for those who look for surface interest. With such handicaps the place more than holds its own amidst the grim contours which form the eternal background ; it is, however, friendly and kindly in expression to those inclined to investigate its humours. It lacks the warmth and snugness of close packing. There are no slums, neither is there that element of antique mystery, the chief asset of towns of great age.

Placed by artifice high above everyday things it courts the wildest weather, the winds that blow, the mists that damp and the rains that sting. Summer on these heights begins late and finishes early, the change of the seasons is noted by the traveller climbing the road up from Plymouth, or in the coaches of the diminutive train that crawls around the hills amidst granite boulders like a centipede on a benevolent mission.

Aloof and separate, enthroned amidst the splendour of skyscape and eternal hills, swept by the elements and warmed by the sun, at times blotted out by fog and wheezing like an asthmatic in the rarefied air, the town manages to preserve its attitude of kindly nonchalance. But it has previously been written that the place is upstart and uncongenial, how then that it be receptive and friendly ? The reason is not hard to seek ; all things go by contrasts, as those who have tramped the moorland roads know to their everlasting gratitude. Even the ponies make for the town's shelter when the weather can no longer be sustained, there to find scant comfort under porch and pent or on the lee side of a stone wall. From some points the sentinel mass of the church tower is the dominant note ; from others the not unpleasant radiation of the prison buildings, accented by grated windows by day and at night pricked with iridescent points, from the focal point in the local hub. Whatever its intrinsic merits or demerits as a town, under such conditions and in such a situation the friendliness of the plain houses is unmistakable.

Thomas Tyrwhitt, to whom Princetown owes its origin, appears in the paintings of him, which are extant, to have been a very handsome man. He was born in 1762, was educated at Eton and eventually passed to Christchurch, Oxford, where he took his B.A. degree in 1784. Tyrwhitt owed his introduction to the Prince of Wales to Dr. Cyril Jackson, and from this start can be traced his subsequent career, first as private secretary to the Prince and to the Council and at a later date auditor to the Duchy of Cornwall. For many years he lived in the household of the Prince of Wales, having a special suite assigned to him at Carlton House. That he had regard for the modes of the princely court, and taste for the work of Henry Holland, to whom the embellishment of Carlton House in the first instance had been entrusted, before the furnishing was spoilt by Walsh Porter, is evidenced by the fact that, when Carlton House was removed to make way for Nash's improvements, Sir Thomas Tyrwhitt secured some of the painted doors and at least two of the marble fireplaces to reuse at Tor Royal.

Tyrwhitt's knowledge of Dartmoor began about the year 1785, the result of personal investigation while engaged in Duchy business. For the purpose of enclosing moorland and laying out a farm with outbuildings and a dwelling-house for his own use, Tyrwhitt selected a site within the Forest betwixt Prince Hall and Two Bridges enclosures on the one side and the Walkhampton Commons on the other. Following tradition, he wisely selected a sheltered valley site. This farmhouse, which he named Tor Royal, was finished in 1798, and it was here that he spent his spare time, making the long journey from London by chaise, and after much painful labour having roads formed across the moorland, much as they are to-day, for wheeled traffic. A man of indefatigable industry, living at a time when agriculture was a passion with the aristocracy and when activity of this sort required herculean endeavours, he spared neither time nor money to realise his ideal. The fact is, Tyrwhitt was a visionary. What Francis, the fifth Duke of Bedford, was doing for Bedfordshire in the neighbourhood of Woburn, and Samuel Whitbread at Southill and the adjacent villages, Tyrwhitt contemplated excelling in the wilds of Dartmoor. His first thought was the reclamation of land, the second the improvement of old trackways and the forming of new, while his dreams ultimately led him to create a market-town and to bring a railway from Plymouth to a wharf within half a mile of his own house. He named the town after his royal patron, and the first building, the oldest now standing, an inn, was called the " Plume of Feathers." There is a paragraph in the *Bristol Review* of the 13th July, 1805, which states :

" The Prince of Wales is about to erect at his own expense a chapel at Prince Town in the Forest of Dartmoor, under the direction of Thomas Tyrwhitt, Esq., Lord Warden of the Stannaries. Mr. Tyrwhitt has suggested to Government the propriety of erecting a building near the above for depositing such prisoners of war as may be brought into Plymouth ; who can without difficulty be conveyed up the River Tamar and landed a few miles from the spot. It is said this plan will be acted upon forthwith, and barracks built for the reception of a proportionate number of troops."

On the 18th of July, 1805, a new character appears at Tor Royal in the person of Daniel Asher Alexander, the architect who, in company with Tyrwhitt, visited several sites in the vicinity in order to select one suitable for building the prison. Six months later the plans were ready, for a letter now written by Mr. Tyrwhitt on behalf of the Prince of Wales states that a lease would be granted of 390 acres for the purpose desired.

Alexander was not the least among the architect-engineers who flourished at the beginning of the last century. His works can be traced in various parts of England, mainly structures of utility, inland and along the coasts, evidencing his skill as a designer and constructor. Pre-eminently a Londoner, he eventually transferred his activities to Exeter and the west country, equally able to plan a lighthouse out in the deeps or to prepare a scheme for turning the scattered rocks of the Scillies into a formidable naval base. His portrait by Masquerier shows a benevolent face with a high forehead, searching eyes and humorous mouth. It is a face typical of the professional man of the period, that of one confident in his power to create lasting works, to take command of others and denoting rare ability to organise. In London Alexander formed one of a coterie of artists and architects : his intimate friends were Flaxman and Chantrey, in whose company, after 1815, he made annual trips to France, travelling by diligence from province to province to gather ideas. In common with other men of the time, he made his journeys on horseback or by chaise, he carried a copy of *Paterson's Roads*, the *Bradshaw* of coaching days, was respected by the skippers of the Calais packets, and lived to see the victories of Trevithick and Stephenson. In the meantime, his lighthouses were guiding the mariner at Harwich, Heligoland, Holyhead, Lundy, the Ferne Islands, and the Bishops. His docks berthed Indiamen, his wharves sloops and lighters, his warehouses held the country's principal imports, his bridges carried their loads and his prisons throbbed with the emotions of thousands, for it fell to Alexander's lot to build the granite stronghold on Dartmoor and later the jail at Maidstone. Should the Corporation of the City of London need expert assistance Alexander was called in, his skill was courted by the London Dock Company and by the Admiralty Board, and as Surveyor to the Trinity Brethren his tasks were multifarious.

Much has been recorded of the privations suffered by the French and American prisoners of war who underwent the rigours of detention on the bleak heights of Dartmoor, their sufferings have become part of local tradition. There is sufficient of the architect's masterpiece still standing to explain the character of his work, for like Dance's Newgate the prison was a product of stern necessity. No blame attaches to the architect for the imperfections of the accommodation ; the problem he faced was in every way novel, his realisation of the idea had all the imagination and mystery of a Piranesian fantasy, and by such methods he expressed the iron will of the England of our forebears.

It is of interest to refer to particulars of the upbringing of such a man. Daniel Asher Alexander was born in London in the year 1768 and at an early age entered St. Paul's School; when fourteen years old he was allowed to follow his natural bent as a designer, and about this time he became a student at the Royal Academy, where he listened to the teachings of Thomas Sandby. Such was his application that within two months he obtained a silver medal. The immediate effect of this initial success was that his father articled him to a Mr. Samuel Robinson, then practising in Finsbury Circus, where the boy became familiar with the principles of heavy construction then in vogue for warehouses, which formed the basis of his chief's practice. From the foregoing will be understood how such early training fitted him for his future work as an architect-engineer. In those days, as now, the training of an architect was deemed to be a matter of slow purpose and pupilage of five years a mere preliminary to more serious application.

Alexander as a youth had such confidence in his power to create that directly his term of five years' apprenticeship ceased he engaged to build a house for a Doctor Saunders on Highbury Hill, a district then rapidly developing. This work was completed to the satisfaction of the client. In rapid succession followed commissions for warehouses at Bankside and in Mark Lane. It is about this nucleus of his extensive practice that all his subsequent eminence centres. At that period, while still in the early 'twenties, he advised the Trinity Brethren upon the widening of Rochester Bridge, an undertaking of extreme hazard in which it was necessary to form two central arches into one. Alexander made his plans and proceeded to form caissons, but as fast as the new piers were built the swift tide cleared the cement until the existence of the whole structure was threatened. In his preliminary report the young architect had advised the authorities that it would be essential to keep the pumps going seven days a week without cessation, but the Trinity officials had scruples regarding the strict observance of the Sabbath. At last, when disaster seemed inevitable, wiser counsels prevailed, the contract was finished and the bridge as altered stood for years.

In 1796 Alexander was appointed Surveyor to the London Dock Company and was instructed to prepare a survey of the site for the proposed docks, the completed plans for which were ready in seventy days. In the years that followed his work chiefly centred upon the construction of lighthouses, until at the time when the Treaty of Amiens ceased to be he was a man still young but at the zenith of his reputation.

Napoleon could make preparation for the invasion of England and could issue his mandates, but sea power ruled otherwise. The Channel was swept, French shipping cleared and ship-to-ship actions fought until Trafalgar removed the menace. All the while prisoners taken in the naval actions crowded the prisons improvised in haste at Norman Cross, near Peterborough, and Stapleton, near Bristol, the prison hulks at Plymouth and Chatham were held by the French to be atrocious and home opinion was dismayed by the evils of overcrowding. It became apparent that a special establishment was urgently required ; at this juncture the Transport Board, then attached to the Admiralty, applied to Mr. Tyrwhitt, Secretary to the Duchy of Cornwall, regarding the site for a prison on Dartmoor ; the consent of the Prince of Wales was obtained and as soon as arrangements could be made the work under Alexander was started. It was Tyrwhitt's one ambition to reclaim some portion of Dartmoor Forest for agricultural purposes. In this he was the object of local contempt, although as a member of Parliament for Plymouth he was respected. The choice of Dartmoor must in the first place have been suggested by him, especially as it fitted in with his own views of local development.

Tyrwhitt's knowledge of building conditions on Dartmoor were of extreme use to Alexander, who, as previously mentioned, was introduced by a member of the Transport Board to the Secretary at Tor Royal and in his company " examined a variety of situations suitable for prison building, and fixed at length upon a place near Mr. Tyrwhitt's lodges." From reliable data it is safe to assume that Mr. Tyrwhitt had already decided upon the site most suitable to assist in the development of his pet scheme, namely Princetown. Alexander with characteristic energy surveyed the ground, noted the levels and the water supply, took stock of the abundance of granite ready for building material, mounted his horse and returned through Exeter to London, where he proceeded to prepare the plans illustrated. The architect's first calculation of the cost, some £86,243 13s. 4d., as all preliminary estimates are wont to do, completely upset the economical view of the Board, so that he was asked to prepare a second and less ambitious scheme. The scheme finally chosen included five prison buildings capable of holding a thousand men each, a hospital, petty officers' prison and barracks for five hundred troops. At that time the Government was in monetary difficulties. It was obvious, even to those who wished otherwise, that the war would go on indefinitely, and in addition there were labour difficulties that presented almost insuperable obstacles. Alexander's organising powers at once came into action. His first order was to import masons from Yorkshire, but it was not long before he reported that "the Masons in the country are beginning to rouze," and that Cornwall could supply men of ability at reduced wages.

The works were begun, and after four years of incessant toil, during which time the contractors were thoroughly disheartened and almost bankrupt, the prison was completed, and on the 24th of May, 1809, the first batch of prisoners some 2500 strong was marched up from Plymouth. A month later the buildings held the full complement of 5000 for which they had been projected, but the establishment was not finally in full order until three years later.

The illustration on page 139, taken from Ackermann's *Repository* for 1810, illustrates the prison as originally designed by Alexander. It is a plan drawn in quasi-perspective. It shows the radial system devised by the architect, which subsequently became the system followed throughout the nineteenth century for prison design ; there are the boundary walls, the reservoir and the entrance gateway still extant. Alexander, like most of his contemporaries, had a collection of Piranesan outpourings , including the " Carceri d'Invenzione," a series of especial interest to him as a constructor. His care for such things is seen in the design of the main granite gateway with its shouldered arch and sunk panel bearing the inscription in Roman capitals " PARCERE SUBJECTIS." Not only did Alexander's task include the building of the war prison, but he schemed the houses for the numerous officials connected with the establishment, many of which stand to-day. These include the cottages in the main street at Princetown above the church, the Duchy Hotel, now altered and added to, the Governor's and the Chaplain's houses and other works.

Between the years 1811 and 1815 he superintended the building of the Church of St. Michael and the vicarage, employing masons from among the French prisoners for the fabric, and carpenters from among the Americans for the carpentry. Many have been the alterations to his curious "Gothick" church since that time, but the tower, the main walls and the windows are intact. The plans illustrated give a fair idea of the scope of the work as well as direct evidence of the nucleus of Princetown, Tyrwhitt's pet scheme at the close of the struggle with Napoleon. It is fascinating to think of Alexander setting out the outlines of Dartmoor prison on his mahogany elephant table with the grim assurance of one determined to put Piranesian rhetoric into practice. Little could he have thought, even in his most imaginative moments, that it would be peopled by creatures as fantastic as those limned on the copper-plate by the Italian, but he came to understand the temperament of the crowd of destitute men, known as " Romans," who fought like animals for their food and at times half naked survived the winters of Dartmoor, although some were less fortunate. But the prison as a hold for foreign soldiers and sailors was nearing its end, for from July the 26th to August 8th, 1815, Napoleon himself was viewing the heights of Dartmoor from the deck of a British ship in Plymouth Sound, and seven months later the last of the prisoners had been repatriated, the gates were locked and the buildings left to decay.

Long before the ending of the Napoleonic wars the idea of commuting the prison into a penal establishment for convicts, in lieu of transportation to Botany Bay, was in contemplation, for the continued prosperity of Princetown became Sir Thomas Tyrwhitt's immediate care. He it was who conceived the idea of employing convict labour for the reclamation of Dartmoor as an agricultural centre, and, when the war ended, he was the first to appreciate the then modern theory of a railroad. The latter was projected about the year 1819 and completed in 1823. From the time the prisoners of war moved out until the first batch of convicts moved in under the new system from Millbank thirty-seven years passed, the buildings had to be repaired and altered, and those who had witnessed the early realisation of such a huge structure in such an inaccessible position had passed away.

Alexander's works are legion and entitle him to rank as a scientific constructor of the status of Brindley, Telford, and the Rennies at a time when architectural engineering was in its infancy. Eighteenth-century ecleticism was still in favour of exploiting all known styles in the pursuit of novelty of design and, although Alexander had recourse to all published works on building and mixed with the leading artists, he allowed nothing to influence his opinions that did not admit of ready translation into terms of local material and in accordance with local traditions and customs. Imbued with the sense of his own power, he nevertheless understood his limitations and was ever ready to listen to the opinions of others. His clients numbered most of the leading men in England, hence the scope of his practice, which included works representative of every type. He was meticulous to a degree in the preservation of old work, but his great force inhered in his ability to scheme original and daring methods of construction.

Once, when called upon to give expert evidence in the Courts of Law, he completely upset the opposing counsel, James Scarlett, who went out of his way to upset the architect's opinion. The case being argued was connected with some extensive building works. Scarlett's opening question was : " Your occupation is that of a builder ? " " I am more than that," was the reply, " I am an architect." " What is the difference, Mr. Architect or Mr. Builder ? " retorted Scarlett. " There is a slight distinction," Alexander replied. " A builder supplies material and the

L

architect gives the brains." " Very well," snapped Scarlett, now irate. " Perhaps you will inform the Court from your mighty intelligence who was the architect for the Tower of Babel ? " Alexander instantly replied : " There was no architect ; hence the confusion."

Alexander was a product of that most interesting period the transition between the late eighteenth and the early nineteenth centuries, the period that carried earlier customs from one epoch to another, that brought the blind force of steam into being and gave this country the respite from years of warfare as well as impetus to the reorganisation of social and political matters. From the study of these two men, Tyrwhitt and Alexander, much can be gleaned respecting the life of the times now just receding into obscurity—the influence of the patron who acted for the Prince of Wales, and the labours of the architect who crystallised the vision of the far-seeing patron into terms of building that is still eloquent of other days, the one so essential to the other. Much had been done by architects in the opening years of Alexander's career to raise taste to the academic platform, his bent, on the other hand, while not opposed to polite expression, had in its essence something of the scale of the works of the Roman military builders, and the distinction that sometimes his duties carried him out to the deeps, there to plant beacons on dangerous reefs and to add to the miracle of safe navigation.

Many other incidents of his career can be supplied, details of his life in London, the gifts bestowed upon him by grateful clients, his readiness of wit, the domestic charm of his home in the city of Exeter and his desire to be buried in the churchyard at Yarmouth in the Isle of Wight, the tower of which he had erected at his own charge, the better to point out the seaway. He belonged to the old group of architect-engineers now unfortunately almost extinct ; his life was most useful and happy. The joy is that the majority of his works still testify to his fame.

People in England are fast adjusting their views to the true meaning of architecture ; no longer is it regarded as belonging to an esoteric order of things, something mysterious and beyond the ken of ordinary discussion. There is a wiser conception of the purport of building irrespective of archæology and the lavish display of ornament. Princetown, the plainest of towns, while it does not possess the antiquity of places of more ancient development, has a character entirely its own, that is to say, the older parts of the place. There is a simplicity of purpose in its aspect almost Spartan in character, a directness of purpose aiding the expression that has a charm of its own and an interest of association bound up with a strenuous experience in national affairs.

CHAPTER IX

THE ISLES OF SCILLY

AN ACCOUNT OF HUGH TOWN AND THE BUILDINGS ON ST. MARY'S

THE Isles of Scilly comprise six large islands with attendant islets and groups of rocks numbering approximately a hundred and forty-five. They stand twenty-eight miles off Land's End and are of a beauty and charm enhanced by the wildness and isolation of the setting. Their characteristics are those of Cornwall in miniature, and the same can be said of the

HOUSES AT HUGH TOWN, ST. MARY'S, ISLES OF SCILLY.
Early nineteenth century.

buildings, to the making of which the traditions of the mainland have in part contributed. St. Mary's is the largest of the islands, and here is concentrated the architectural interest.

It is conjectured that early Greek navigators first discovered the islands and gave them the name of the Hesperides and that the Phœnicians called them the " Cassiterides," or tin islands, later renamed by the Romans " Siluræ Insulæ." The earliest mention of the Isles in English history appears to have been in the

147

early part of the tenth century, when they were granted by Athelstan to some monks who settled at Tresco. In the reign of Edward the First the remainder of the islands became royal property, and from thenceforward were held on lease at a rental of so many puffins annually until the reign of Queen Elizabeth, when they were divided among numerous proprietors, from whom they were eventually purchased by the Crown, but from the late sixteenth century until 1830 they were rented by the Godolphin family. Such is a synopsis of the historical facts. Of the Abbey at Tresco little remains but some fragments of the arcading, but as previously mentioned St. Mary's is by no means deficient in regional buildings.

HUGH TOWN, ST. MARY'S, ISLES OF SCILLY. STORM PORCH. 1812.

At Hugh Town, the capital, there is much of interest. There is Star Castle on the height above the town, built in 1593 as a measure of protection against a second invasion from Spain; there is the Georgian garrison, the pier built in 1601, and the historic "Pool" or harbour; there are the various towers and telegraph stations of other times. Some of the older stone buildings in the town go back to Elizabethan days. The isles are particularly rich in historical associations. Under Sir John Grenville, the royalist, renowned as a participant in the restoration of Charles the Second, they were fortified in 1644 and formed a base for the privateers which swept the seas until the Roundheads despatched Admiral Blake and Sir George Ayscue two years later to compel surrender. Then were fired the only shots that menaced the Elizabethan fort. It was on a treacherous part of St. Mary's coast that Sir Cloudesley Shovel, commanding a portion of the British fleet, was lost during the night of October 22nd, 1707, when two thousand seamen perished with the Admiral; a fragment of his ship, *The Association*, is preserved in the Parish Church.

Star Castle, a prominent landmark, stands about one hundred feet above sea-level; it is built entirely of granite, and soon after completion, notwithstanding the ingenuity of its design, was considered obsolete. It was here that the fugitive Charles the Second, when Prince of Wales, took refuge and complained of the loneliness of the place and the vile accommodation.

Immediately below the Castle is the Garrison, the entrance to which is at the north-east end above the Pool. Over the entrance is a stone panel with the initials

HUGH TOWN, ST. MARY'S, ISLES OF SCILLY. THE STEWARD'S HOUSE.
DETAIL OF PARLOUR. 1730.

HOUSES NEAR THE PARADE, HUGH TOWN, ST. MARY'S, ISLES OF SCILLY. 1815.

L *

G.R. 1742 A.T.; the last letters evidently the signature of one Abraham Tovey, a master gunner, under whose direction the works were reconstructed and improved when George the Second was king. Abraham Tovey was an engineer of no mean ability, for he projected and formed the excellent roads that completely encircle the Garrison. It is evident that the master gunner of Georgian times went to some pains to take out the earlier Elizabethan panel in order to record the activities of his own time. Over the entrance to the Garrison is a bell which was formerly rung at three, six, and nine in the evening and struck at the termination of the intermediate hours.

HUGH TOWN, ST. MARY'S, ISLES OF SCILLY. HOUSE AT FOOT
OF GARRISON HILL. 1800.

Star Castle itself is one of the most perfect Elizabethan structures in existence; in plan it exhibits eight salients projecting twenty-five feet, and on every point is a watch house, although two have partly fallen to ruin. The roofs of the latter rising immediately above the walls.

A platform seven feet high and seven feet wide connects the whole of the interior work and this is surmounted by a wall or breastwork nearly the same height, each angle of which is pierced with loopholes for musketry.

The height of the walls on the outside from the ditch is about eighteen feet. Within the outer works is a dwelling-house which corresponds in shape to the stellar

HUGH TOWN, ST. MARY'S, ISLES OF SCILLY. STUCCOED HOUSE, NEAR THE PARADE. 1820.

HUGH TOWN, ST. MARY'S, ISLES OF SCILLY. SMALL HOUSE. PERIOD 1797.

formation. The house is separated from the outer works by a sort of fosse about four feet across. The rooms in the lower part of the house are of basement character and have little interest save for the large room which in former days did duty as a mess-room for the garrison. Here is to be seen a magnificent granite fireplace of Elizabethan date. The height of the wall from the base court is about twenty-one feet, a third of which lies below the platform, another third is hidden by the breast-work and the remainder with its peaked roof is just seen above the battlements.

EXTERIOR OF STAIRCASE AND PORCH OVER LOW ENTRY, HUGH TOWN, ST. MARY'S,
ISLES OF SCILLY. 1810.

The house was in former times intended to be the residence of the Military Commandant.

The castle is entered by a small stone bridge thrown over the dry ditch, and passes beneath a small tower which has grooves for an armoured portcullis. The tower formerly carried a bell, over the entrance are the letters

E.R.

1593

At one time the improved " garrison " of George the Second's day could boast

HOUSES NEAR THE PARADE, HUGH TOWN, ST. MARY'S, ISLES OF SCILLY. 1800.

SHOP WINDOW CONVERSION TO A HOUSE ON THE PARADE. 1820.
HUGH TOWN, ST. MARY'S, ISLES OF SCILLY.

eighteen battlements and bastions ; it was calculated to protect the town, the Hugh and the bays, as well as to dispute the passage of the Sound. These bastions were connected by curtain walls, each about fifty-two yards in length and each having an embrasure in the centre.

As previously mentioned, Hugh Town is the principal town in the island, and it is to a study of its buildings that attention must at this point be directed.

The town which developed beneath the shadow of the garrison and in proximity to the Pool grew from a small collection of fishermen's cottages until it displaced the pretensions of Old Town. It is in the main situated partly on a low sandy

HUGH TOWN, ST. MARY'S, ISLES OF SCILLY. MRS. MUMFORD'S SHOP. 1828.

peninsula which joins St. Mary's to the hill, called the Hugh, now known as the Garrison, and partly at the bottom of the hill as well as on the slopes. It has one principal street, a pleasant central space called the Parade, and many odd runaways to the water's edge. The principal street is about 320 yards long, it is irregular in its course and pleasing in its severity and tidiness. The houses are constructed of local granite, but the foundations upon which the massive walls rest are shallow, in some places not more than eighteen inches below the footway. Hugh Town has but few shops, but it can point to a fair assemblage of inns. At the north end of the principal street is the old pier or quay with attendant storehouses. The pier is slightly newer than the castle and was first built in 1601 and underwent repairs

GROUP OF HOUSES IN HIGH STREET. 1785-1800. HUGH TOWN,
ST. MARY'S, ISLES OF SCILLY.

A GENTEEL HOUSE, HUGH TOWN, ST. MARY'S, ISLES OF SCILLY. 1810.

and additions between the years 1749 and 1751, when its measurements extended to 430 feet long and about twenty in breadth.

One of the most interesting houses in the town is that called the Steward's House, a replica in miniature of a Cornish manor house of the first part of the eighteenth century. It is substantially built of granite and can show the original wooden railings in excellent preservation. Internally the house is beautifully finished, the rooms are panelled and the fireplaces characteristic of the period.

A SMALL HOUSE. 1815.   TYPICAL DOOR TRIM. 1815.
HUGH TOWN, ST. MARY'S, ISLES OF SCILLY.

No trace can now be seen of the fine mulberry trees that formerly graced the garden at the back.

Over a century since, when Alexander, the architect, was preparing his famous scheme for a breakwater which would turn the Sound into a naval base for the British fleet, the appearance of Hugh Town was much the same as it is to-day, save for the fact that thatch was more commonly used to cover the roofs. Even at this period tiles were in use as well as small slates, but the gales of a century have done much to destroy these materials. Most of the smaller houses at that time were covered with thatch laid on in a peculiar manner. Owing to the prevalence of westerly gales, especially from the vernal to the autumnal equinox, the people had, it appears, recourse to certain methods for securing the thatch. For this purpose large wooden pegs were driven into the crevices between the masonry about a foot and a half from the top of the walls and at a little distance from each other. When thatch of sufficient thickness was in position it was bound down with straw-plaited ropes, which in turn were tied to the wooden pegs. The binding thus extended from the front to the back of the houses. The effect, which can still be judged from a few remaining thatched roofs, is not unpleasant. The characteristics of the houses can best be seen from the illustrations. The majority are two storeys in height, but a few run to three storeys. The granite masonry is worked with extreme care, the windows have outside frames and good fan-lights to the doors. In some examples bow windows have been added.

The Steward's House is perhaps the most interesting from the standpoint of interior finish, as can be judged from the illustration showing the fireplace and panelling to one of the first-floor rooms. The date of this house is about 1730. The smaller houses, such as the one at the foot of the hill to the Garrison, date from about 1790, and rely for their effect on the texture of the masonry and the harmony that exists between the wall surface and the windows. Other types of the early nineteenth century form part of terrace groupings, such as those on the south side of the Parade.

The joinery, as shown in the detail of bow windows and door-panels, is exceptionally good, and together with the variety shown in the design of the door-knockers, of which several examples have been selected for illustration, proves that as much attention was given to such minor features for small houses as would be bestowed on buildings of greater scale and pretension. Some of the larger houses have, in addition to balancing bay windows, ornate trellis-work to the central

CHIPPENDALE PERIOD CHAIR AT STAR CASTLE.
HUGH TOWN, ST. MARY'S, ISLES OF SCILLY.
The property of H.R.H. the Prince of Wales.

doorway; these in general can be attributed to the years that followed Waterloo. There are also a few examples of conversion of parlours to serve as shops, such as the one on the Parade dating from 1820. A typical late-Georgian shop-front is Mrs. Mumford's in the High Street, a pleasant survival of the period which approved the sashing of windows into small squares. This shop-front in the near future is to be reconstructed on the old lines in a new position.

Of the influence of the later classic movements in vogue on the mainland, and mainly emanating from Plymouth, Truro, and Penzance, much can be said.

There is an excellent specimen of a storm-porch to a house at the south end of Hugh Town (see page 148), which is constructed of wood with three-way doors.

The motif of the design is a free treatment of Doric pilasters ; this triple-door treatment belongs to the period of the Regency and proclaims the influence of the works of Foulston at Plymouth. Another late example, as characteristic in its simplicity as the Steward's House, is the stuccoed house beyond the south end of the Parade. It is also interesting to note that the builders of over a century ago could produce picturesque effects if occasion, as well as planning conditions, demanded something out of the ordinary. For instance, the treatment of the external staircase and porch above a low entry has an exceptional and forceful character ; particularly happy is the treatment of the iron balustrade both in style and detail (see page 152).

Building in the Isles of Scilly of the period discussed has an independent and articulate expression, but it owes no small part of its finesse to mainland influences. The small houses, cottages, and tenements at Hugh Town stand close set, partly a legacy from the early days when mutual protection against attack was the first essential, but more precisely because the scale of everything has to accord with the natural scale of St. Mary's. There are no large houses on St. Mary's, neither do large ships enter the Sound nor the Pool. Here and there off the High Street in Hugh Town can be observed a house of larger size than usual standing attic height above its neighbour, or, as in the case of the Steward's House and two of the later Regency houses, assuming an unusual importance. Throughout the eighteenth century the people of St. Mary's and the neighbouring isles were engaged in smuggling, fishing, or privateering. A few it is certain took a watch on shore to tend the land ; it was not, however, until after the Napoleonic wars, when the Admiralty and the Revenue men exercised their authority in a rigorous sense, that farming for export became a reality.

The miniature scale of the houses has been previously mentioned. Here, too, is matter for further enquiry ; the majority are of late eighteenth-century date and

DETAIL OF A FRONT DOOR.
HUGH TOWN, ST. MARY'S, ISLES OF SCILLY.

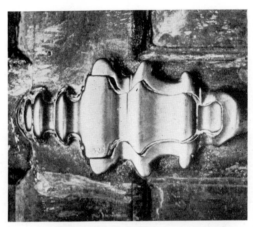

TYPICAL DOOR KNOCKERS. HUGH TOWN, ST. MARY'S, ISLES OF SCILLY.

bear the same relation to houses of similar class in Cornwall as a sloop of the period did to a small brig. At first glance the long, low grey terracings appear to have little interest, but from the windows many strange faces have peered and from the doors, armed with cutlass and pistols, have issued forth men accustomed to stop at nothing. Small as the houses are and built as they were by men of simple outlook, they have served their purpose and are still as serviceable as when first built.

The Scillonian of the past, who was equally at home on the face of the waters as on the land, was also a master builder. He could appraise the qualities of worked granite, which he took a pride in quarrying and shaping; he could thatch to suit the climate and sheet down his reeding as tautly as he could reef a topsail. When funds permitted, following a bold venture to the French coast, he would order a cargo of Cornish slates, smalls by preference, with which to cover the new house. There is further evidence of the pride taken by the Scillonians in their houses in the presence of the hob and other grates of Carron manufacture which became essential when the colliers from Newcastle took in St. Mary's as well as Penzance. And at this time it is conjectured Soho and Birmingham catered for seaport and island taste in the matter of brass door-knockers and other furniture.

REGENCY FIREPLACE IN HALL. 1810.
HUGH TOWN, ST. MARY'S, ISLES OF SCILLY.

Regarding the interior of the houses and cottages these are comparatively low and suggest the proportions of the 'tween decks of a frigate, a resemblance maintained by the worked floor-joists and the close-fitted boarding of the floor over, for plaster ceilings were avoided as much as possible for technical reasons. Such facts as the foregoing go far to explain the simplicity of the Scillonian style, which had little use for ornamental externals, save those which could be imported easily. The Scillonians were forced by necessity to invent ornament of their own fashioning. But the spell of the eighteenth century, its self-sufficiency, its mock gentility, its surface respectability and good-nature infuses the whole of the miniature buildings on the islands. There is to be seen concrete evidence of the whims of mainland taste. There is expressed the mind of contemporary natives to be thought every whit as proper men as the foreigners in Cornwall and, to attain this, they spared no pains to embellish their houses externally with door-trims and fanlights and to fit up the parlour and the kitchen with the compactness of the cabins of the ships they looked upon as live things. Such are a few of the charms of traditional buildings in the isles. It is a form of expression foreign to the lamp of the architect, it is elusive to describe, yet it is, in spite of its standoffishness, singularly attractive and engaging to enquiry.

The people of the past, the master masons, slaters, and carpenters, not only shaped the materials but gave their creations a certain Promethean fire ; they contrived to fit houses to men and families, so that once rooted a family would be in no hurry to move from the paternal hearth. Here is the secret : it is one of structure, not of design or construction, not of ornament or booky lore, but one that is inherent in man, emotional and instinctive, the power of conceiving and imparting.

M

CHAPTER X

CONCLUSION

NO account of the later building development in Devon and Cornwall would be complete without a summary of the natural materials which form part of the physical structure of the country and in turn provide material for the buildings.

From the east side of Dartmoor begins the granite ridge which continues, with various interruptions, to form the backbone of Cornwall, until it stops precipitately at Land's End and reappears in the Isles of Scilly. In the west country this granitic formation can be regarded as the fundamental material of the whole region. Nearly all the finely worked granite which in the nineteenth century was used by architects and engineers in London was obtained from the boulders of Dartmoor, Cheesewring and Penryn. Sir John Rennie used it for the Victualling Yard at Stonehouse, as well as for facing the Breakwater across Plymouth Sound. It was used for Waterloo and London Bridges, and by Laing for the Customs House at Plymouth. In the rough it forms the basic material for the walls of houses on Dartmoor and throughout Cornwall ; but it is treacherous in one respect, for it admits of the penetration of moisture through the earthy part of the stone despite all precautions taken in the construction. Haytor on Dartmoor and Kit Hill in Cornwall are two of the principal eastern sites where granite is found in situ and is most readily quarried and transported. The hardness and tenacity of the material varies from that which blunts the steel implement to that which breaks under a sharp blow, or that in a state of decomposition, which can be worked through with a spade. There are also the numerous local sandstones akin to Totternhoe stone in Bedfordshire, the limestone conglomerates and marbles. In addition there is Dunstone or Shillet as well as the numerous slatey formations, whitish, greeny-grey, and red.

If Cornwall is considered primarily a mining county, Devonshire occupies the premier position as an agricultural one ; both are noted for intensive cultivation, but the palm falls to Devon.

To-day the roads, at all times important to farming, are in first-class order ; this was not the case a hundred years since. In the seventeenth century they were both rough and unpleasant. The turnpike roads came into being about the middle of the eighteenth century, but it was not until the beginning of the nineteenth that road improvements on the grand scale were undertaken in the west country. Then, by levelling hills, building up causeways and making direct lines in place of the narrow windings, transport was made comparatively easy. To this period most of the slated toll-houses on the western roads can be ascribed.

From the earliest times the cultivated lands were enclosed by fences of earth and stones, or stonewalling built dry. They were intended to form an obstacle to cattle and by their height to give shade and protection from wind and rain to growing crops. Of the way in which the distribution of land came about little is known. The farms and holdings have developed quite naturally through the centuries, but in general they have originally been small in size, until in time two or three have been brought together as the property of one owner. The farms in Devonshire have the distinction of forming centres by themselves, with the homestead as a

THE MARKET HALL, TRURO. 1846. GRANITE BUILT.
Christopher Eales, Architect.

GATE PIER IN GRANITE FROM
NEAR BODMIN MOOR. 1750.

nucleus. In every case the site for the house has been well chosen, either on the side of a valley or on rising ground at the head of a combe or dell, positions equally determined by the requirements of shelter and running water. In Devonshire will be encountered cob or earth walls, sometimes stuccoed over in the case of dwellings, but the out-buildings and the fenced garden walls left untouched to show the earthy nature of the district. From the nucleus of the homestead with its buildings and cottages for the hinds many hamlets have come to be named. In the Devonshire village the use of cob on an extensive scale can be seen, in some cases the cob is reinforced with timbering and the walls are plastered and colour washed. Other farm-houses are of stone and brick with roofs of tile, slate, and thatch. It is the delightful informality of structure that is the most pleasant feature of Devonshire and Cornwall. In the former county picturesqueness results from the fluent lines gained by the free working of materials which are of the earth earthy. In Cornwall there is a certain rigidity of line due to more precise working, in turn occasioned by the limitations of the material.

The foregoing remarks apply to the purely local aspect of the tradition, but both instances afford evidence of the way the native builders by experience arrived at a sense of scale and harmonic proportion independent of rules; it can be said the houses sit well amidst the scenery, they have a native colour and expression, their purpose is obvious and natural. Each of the districts, north, east, south, and west in Devon and Cornwall produced its own building statement for the dwellings of its countryfolk, but provincial ideas were to yield to extraneous theories that descended on the western region in the several ways previously described. Hence the slow merging of the two interests, as well as the eventual change in favour of comparative formality which was engendered by the eighteenth-century spirit. In the

TOLL HOUSE, NEAR TAVISTOCK. 1806.

old days, as now, the result of intensive culture of the land was production greatly in excess of local demands; an outlet was accordingly found for produce in the neighbouring towns. The nineteenth century, however, extended the dairy produce market to the metropolis and to other parts of England. The culture of orchards and the brewing of cider is another aspect of farming in Devonshire. A century ago the cider

TYPE OF SLATED TOLL HOUSE IN CORNWALL.

trade was relatively almost as active as it is to-day, hogsheads from the neighbourhood of Exeter being sent to London, Liverpool, Newcastle, and the Midlands. In 1770 Moretonhampstead became noted for the growth of large quantities of potatoes, which were sold to the people of Plymouth, the market being held at Two Bridges on Dartmoor. The wool of Dartmoor became famous as early as the reign of Edward the First, when manufactures were rare in England, as a result it was exported in bulk.

PENTILLIE ESTATE OFFICE, NEAR CALLINGTON, CORNWALL. 1820.

While on the subject of agriculture Dartmoor again comes into the writing. At one time the purlieus of the forest were devoted to the purposes of the chase, and rangers were appointed. As time went on small-holdings were established, and from these grew up the system of venville parishes; finally we come to the period of the late eighteenth century when various improvements were initiated. The first improvements were connected with the forming of good roads. In 1772 an Act of Parliament was obtained through the activities of a Mr. Turner, then steward to the Duke of Bedford, for a road from Moreton to Tavistock with branches to Ashburton and Plymouth; but, strange as it may seem, strong opposition was made to the scheme by the towns of Bodmin, Launceston, and Okehampton. Other improvers were Mr. Vollans, Sir Francis Buller, Mr. Thomas Sanders, Mr. Gullet, who built the farming part of the house and outbuildings at Prince Hall (formerly an ancient tenement). The slate-fronted house at Prince Hall was built in 1785 by Sir Francis Buller, who built the original portion of the inn at Two Bridges. No other improver of the

Toll House at Hayle

M *

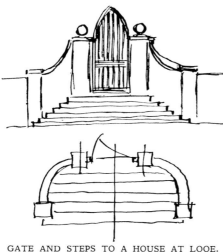

GATE AND STEPS TO A HOUSE AT LOOE.
Early nineteenth century.

time is so prominent as Sir Thomas Tyrwhitt, who began operations in 1785 by reclaiming what was then considered to be the very worst part of the forest. Tor Royal, which is described elsewhere and in the account of Princetown, was begun by Tyrwhitt in 1795, with its fields, plantations, gardens, and stabling. He made the new roads, suggested the building of the war prison, and was indefatigable in the promotion of the railway. The latter was part of Sir Thomas Tyrwhitt's scheme to develop the natural resources of Dartmoor, and in addition to agriculture the promoter had in view the transport of granite for building and engineering purposes. Sir Thomas, having had plans prepared by William Shillibeer (some of the originals are among the archives of the Duchy of Cornwall), attended a meeting of the Plymouth Chamber of Commerce to obtain support for his project; the scheme immediately received approval and the first Act of Parliament for carrying the work out was passed in 1819.

The total length of the line as originally planned was over twenty-five miles. It was opened for traffic in 1823. The railway, however, in its earliest days was not a profitable concern. Subscriptions amounting to £39,983 were obtained and Sir Thomas subscribed over £3000. His interest and enthusiasm for the new method of locomotion is recorded in the frieze of the hall at Tor Royal, which depicts in conventional fashion a repeat ornament showing Trevithick's locomotive drawing a train of trucks with sheaves of wheat between each train. One subscriber, writing twenty years later, states : " The enterprise was a total loss to the subscribers who have not yet, 1839, a shilling dividend." To this and other losses can be ascribed Sir Thomas Tyrwhitt's retirement to Calais. The Dartmoor railroad, now part of the Great Western system, is a remarkable instance of perspicuity on the part of an individual gifted with power to envision the future. Dartmoor at the present time owes its prosperity to the vast schemes of reclamation then undertaken, the railroad was not for the early nineteenth century but for the present, and the proudest hopes of the original projector have been more than realised.

Both Devon and Cornwall have rich mining centres, the history of which begins with the earliest accounts of this country. Through the Middle Ages the mines were not completely worked, but Henry the Seventh apparently gave attention to the revival of the industry. Under Queen Elizabeth monopolies appear to have been granted to foreigners to work the mines. In the time of the Stuarts mining again became active, but the Civil Wars intervened and the workings dwindled until in the reigns of Queen Anne and

WORKED
GRANITE COR-
NICE, TRURO.
1790.

George the First production again increased and was maintained throughout the eighteenth century; in this later prosperity Cornwall principally participated. A century ago the mining industry of Cornwall quickened to new activity: it was then that the beam engine of Trevithick's brain came into play and that the builders and stonemasons bestirred themselves to devise chimney-shafts of approved Doric mould with correct entasis, pedestal, and capping. The great chimney on Kit Hill, near Callington, is a worthy monument to the enterprise of the day, as are the mining villages of Cornwall, which in character are so different from the hamlets of Devonshire. Industrial development in the western region has left its stamp on Cornwall, but it is a mark of silver assay and quite different from the blackness of the Midlands and North country. In Cornwall the great works and pitheads point the heights and give interest to the valleys and undulations. It is a clean industry, as picturesque and inspiring as the furnaces of the North are illusory and depressing. In the buildings of the mining districts of Cornwall mentioned in this work is evidenced the latest expression of regional building and development. The nature of the country has proved its salvation, there are few instances of the spoliation of local amenities or of the growth of industrial centres which could in any sense be deemed of an unsatisfactory type.

Of the other materials which are found and dug, pipe clay, potter's clay, and china clay can be enumerated. There are the rare marbles of Devonshire, such as occur in the lime rocks at Chudleigh, Bickington near Ashburton, Buckfastleigh, Torbay, Babbington, to Drewsteignton, South Tawton, and Yealmpton. In the late eighteenth century a considerable

ROOF TREATMENT TO FARM-HOUSE, NEAR SCORRIER. 1825.

quantity of Babbacombe marble was worked and sent to the makers of chimney-pieces in London. From Chudleigh and Harcombe rocks also came much of the marble for chimney-pieces, not only for Devon and Cornwall houses, but for all parts of England. In this case the material was despatched from the port of Teignmouth.

At this juncture it is convenient to revert to the subject of the coarser building materials. It should be remembered that nearly the whole of the south-western division of Devonshire is famous for its lime works, those at Chudleigh and in the neighbourhood being especially famous. The quarries from whence building stone is obtained comprise Flitton in North Molton, Lew Trenchard, South Tawton, and Beer. The stone from Beer is similar to the old red sandstone of Bedfordshire, from the Totternhoe quarry which is no longer worked. Another material is alabaster, which is procured from the cliffs and used as plaster of Paris.

The slate quarries of Devonshire are as follows: Ivybridge, Cann Quarry, near Plymouth, Lamerton, Lew Trenchard, Millhill and other places near Tavistock, West Alvington, and Buckland Toussaint. It is of interest to note that during the greater part of the eighteenth century up to 1781 large quantities of slate were exported from Buckland to Holland, but the trade was not continued after that date. Slate from the Millhill quarries was exported at this time to Guernsey and Jersey and also to France. In Cornwall the principal slate quarry is the famous one at Delabole.

The fishery interests of both counties also demand attention. There are the river fisheries and the sea fisheries.

Leland mentions Sidmouth as one of the fishing towns of the county and Westcote writes of Plymouth, while Lysons states that fish have been cured on the coast of Devonshire from a very early period. Numerous salt works near the coast are mentioned in the record of Domesday. About the middle of the eighteenth century a brine for curing fish was made at Bideford from rock salt dissolved in sea water, called salt upon salt. Teignmouth, Torbay, and Brixham are all well known as centres of the industry. At the close of the eighteenth century Brixham supplied the markets of Exeter and Bath besides catering for Portsmouth and London. A century ago the oyster beds of Topsham, Starcross, and Lympstone were famous.

Bideford as well as Topsham in the old days enjoyed a considerable trade with Newfoundland, which at a later time was shared by Torquay and Plymouth.

It is the aim of this work to show how closely related architecture is to the prosperity of the two counties, representing as it does the outward expression of countless forces which as a whole make up the social system. Nature has decreed that the chief centres of industry so far as England is concerned shall be in the North.

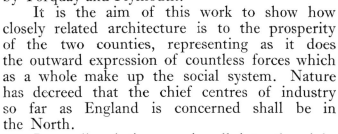

BAY AND CHIMNEY STACKS AT PENZANCE. 1820.

In mediæval times and well into the eighteenth century, as previously mentioned, the woolstapling industry flourished in Devonshire and the neighbouring counties, but eventually prosperity in this regard declined, due to the protracted wars with France and the final struggle with Napoleon. Another cause can be put down to the lack of enterprise among the people of Devonshire and the apathy with which modern invention was regarded. At the beginning of the nineteenth century the woollen industry principally subsisted on the manufacture of serges, which were exported by the East India Company. There can be little doubt that the manufacture of woollens in the western counties was due primarily to the influence of Flanders and the Netherlands, some of the early makers being established at Bristol and Taunton. A wool staple existed in Exeter as early as 1354, and from this date the trade can be said to have started its career. The famous Tostocks, "Tavistock cloths" or "Werstern dozens," were made during the Tudor period. When Queen Elizabeth ruled the trade had grown to considerable magnitude, and the persecutions inflicted on the people of the Netherlands by the Duke of Alva brought hundreds of skilled workers to England and the western counties. Lysons states that the Devonshire kersies had acquired celebrity and were an important article of commerce to the Levant in the early part of the sixteenth century. During the Civil Wars the trade declined, but rose again after the Restoration, principally with Holland ; but after the reign of Queen Anne the export of woollen goods again declined and never recovered, owing to the Dutch preference for the finer materials made in East Anglia. There are frequent references in eighteenth-century literature to the fluctuations of the trade consequent on the wars with France and America. As previously mentioned the trade eventually depended on the good offices of the East India Company.

In the eighteenth century Tiverton could point to a thousand looms in operation. There were large numbers of looms at Newton Bushel, Chudleigh, Bampton, Okehampton, Hatherleigh, Moretonhampstead, Culmstock, and Ottery. Prior to the Napoleonic wars Exeter as well as Crediton, Cullompton and other flourishing places manufactured coarse woollens for Spain, Portugal, Italy, and Germany.

One of the largest centres of the industry was Crediton until the fire which in 1743 destroyed more than half the town. The yarn was spun in Cornwall and in the small towns and villages about Dartmoor and was brought by packhorse to Crediton for weaving. The cloth was then sold to the merchants of Tiverton and Exeter, where it was dyed, pressed and dressed. From Exeter it was sent through Topsham to Holland and the Continent and later to Spain and Italy. In fact, at this period Devon can be said to have clothed the majority of the monks and nuns on the Continent, serges being the material chiefly worn by priests and others. Cullompton also enjoyed a considerable trade with the Continent in serges and druggets. Barnstaple was at one time celebrated for the manufacture of baize as well as, of course, serges for the American colonies.

HOUSE WITH DOUBLE BALCONIES, NEAR PAR. 1830.

Other manufactures in Devonshire include the famous Axminster carpets, first produced in 1755. The old Axminster carpets were produced in one piece of any size or pattern and of any shape. Some are of floral design and others contain armorial bearings or have been woven to accord with the architectural treatment of a room.

Many of the carpets made for Carlton House in the later eighteenth century, to complete Holland's designs for the internal finishing, were made at Axminster. For example, the Pavilion at Brighton was completely furnished with them, as well as the apartments at Windsor and Buckingham Palace.

Honiton lace, or bone lace, was a flourishing industry in the reign of Charles the First, but it eventually gave place to an intensive development of the industry at Nottingham.

In 1816 the large factory at Tiverton, still in operation, was opened by Heathcoat, whose manufactory was originally established in the north until the Luddites destroyed his machines. In the late eighteenth century there was established a factory at Bradiford Bridge for the production of wooden toys, due to the enterprise of a Mr. Furze. It is conceivable that most of the toys shown in the delightful children's books of the time and sold in the toyshops of the seaside watering-places, as well as in London and other cities, were first shaped at Bradiford Bridge.

Devon at this time was also famed for the manufacture of gloves.

Whilst on the subject of local industries the paper mills in the neighbourhood of Exeter have to be noted. Formerly there were three at Bradninch, one of which is in full operation to-day. There were others at Weir and Exeter, at Huxham and Stoke Canon.

Devonshire pottery was made at South Bovey and at Bovey Tracey, where a manufactory of white ware was set up in 1772.

In the eighteenth and early nineteenth centuries Tavistock was noted for its iron-works and foundries. Here the industry centred upon the making of anchors, ships' knees, axles, shovels, scythes, agricultural implements, and tools. Ships' cables were made at Topsham.

Plymouth early in the eighteenth century, under a Mr. Cookworthy, who began to work in 1733, produced a species of porcelain ware, which industry was eventually carried to Bristol and finally to Worcester.

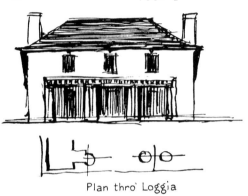

Plan thro' Loggia

URBAN COUNCIL OFFICE, REDRUTH. 1830.

At the beginning of the last century the hackling spinning and weaving of flax for canvas, ducks, sheeting and other coarse linen was a notable feature of the industry of Plymouth ancillary to the requirements of the Navy.

Plymouth's chief industry, the Dockyard, begun, as previously mentioned, in 1691, has since grown to one of the most important naval arsenals in the world.

A century since the principal western ports engaged in commerce were Axminster for coasting vessels; Salcombe for the export of cider and corn and the import of coals; Exeter, the principal export trade being woollen manufactures; Teignmouth, which exported granite, pipe and potter's clay, timber, cider, and fish; Torquay had some part of the Newfoundland trade; Brixham exported fish and imported dried fish from Newfoundland; Plymouth exported copper ore, silver, tin, and lead, as well as antimony from Cornwall, the imports being corn, coals, and foreign produce. A considerable trade was also carried on with North America, the Mediterranean, and the Continent, as well as direct trading with the East Indies. Falmouth long continued, until the advent of steam, to be the port of departure for the American packets. The ports on the northern coast at this time principally engaged in coastal trading.

The rivers of Devon and Cornwall are well known, but they are not of great length, neither are they navigable for more than a few miles, with the exception of the Exe and the Tamar. The canals, on the other hand, are less known, and as these formed a sure and speedy method of transport for heavy materials in the days before railways, a short description is appropriate.

The Exeter Ship Canal is entitled to first place. This is approximately six miles long. Prior to the year 1311 boats and barges came into Exeter along the natural channel of the Exe, but Hugh Courtenay, Earl of Devon, having quarrelled with the Mayor of Exeter, choked up and destroyed the channel of the river below and built two weirs, one of which is called Countess Weir to the present time.

In the reign of Henry the Eighth an Act of Parliament was obtained to remove the obstacles on account of the development of the woollen trade, but this was found to be impossible, so another Act was procured to enable the people of Exeter to cut a canal from the city to the river just above Topsham. The interest of the people in this matter is stated to have been so great that several parishes contributed the church plate to help defray the expense. From time to time the canal was improved, but it was not until Dutch engineers were employed in 1675 that the canal was deepened and made suitable for comparatively large vessels to lie alongside the city quay.

A smaller canal, two and a half miles long, at this time, 1830, connected the navigable part of the river Teign near Newton Bushel with the granite railroad which ran up to Haytor.

HOUSE ON THE QUAY AT STONEHOUSE, PLYMOUTH. 1825.

In 1796 an Act of Parliament was obtained by a private company for making cuts and canals and for otherwise improving the navigation of the Tamar from Morwelham Quay, in the parish of Tavistock, to the vicinity of Launceston; a three-mile length of this canal was completed.

The Tavistock Canal was begun in 1803, also under an Act of Parliament; the canal and tunnels took fourteen years to complete.

The Bude Canal was first surveyed in 1817 and the work was begun in 1819, under the direction of James Green, an engineer of considerable ability. This canal as regards length is one of the most considerable in the western counties. The whole work forms an internal water communication through the counties of Devon and Cornwall of over thirty-five miles. The canal was completed in 1826 at a cost of £128,000 and the original shareholders received no return for their enterprise.

In 1794 John Rennie prepared surveys for his fine project of the Great Western Canal, which was to form a navigable communication from the Bristol Channel to the southern coast. The scheme was to extend from, in the first place, Topsham to Taunton, with branches to Tiverton and Cullompton; the total length of the canal would have been forty-four miles; only twelve miles of the scheme matured, and this section was confined to the centre of the line, which was named the Tiverton or Western Canal. From 1820 onwards the forming of canals engaged the attention of many eminent engineers, including Telford, Rennie, and Green, but many were abandoned after the necessary Act of Parliament had been obtained. Within the next decade the idea of canals gave place to the modern theory of the railroad, beginning with the enterprise in the west country of the group of gentlemen who believed in the far-seeing visions of Sir Thomas Tyrwhitt.

To-day the question of Regional Development as a wider aspect of town planning is one of urgency. In the past, when the population was relatively small, little heed was paid to the subject except in cities, towns, and ports, and then only in a tentative way. It will be understood that in the seventeenth and eighteenth centuries the trunk roads were far from perfect, distances under such conditions appeared immoderately great ; matters, however, underwent considerable change after the passing of the Mail Coach Act and the subsequent improvement of the trunk roads.

Later on, when the miracle of steam came into force, the theoretical scale of the country was diminished, and from that time to this present, when road travel is advancing to a status heretofore unrealised, regional characteristics throughout England have become more general.

In the opening chapter of this book a short description occurs regarding the influence of the contemporary building in the metropolis after the Restoration, and the fact of the transit of the style to Devon and Cornwall along the western arteries. Here it is opportune to write of the local roads of Devon and Cornwall and to reflect on the importance of such in the formation of the broad version of the English Renaissance associated with the people of the west country, which began with the reign of Queen Elizabeth and continued well into the Victorian era.

SHOP TERMINATING IN TERRACE
AT HAYLE. 1840.

The old road books, among which *Britannia Depicta* is the foremost, are insistent and loquacious on the subject of Cities, Borough towns, Antiquity, Charters, Privileges, and Trade, and constitutes reliable gazetteers for the study in hand. Ogilby, for example, deals with the road from London to Land's End and traces the accepted route through Brentford, Staines, Hartley Row, Basingstoke, Andover, Salisbury, Shaftesbury, Sherborne, Axminster, Honiton, Exeter, Chudleigh, Ashburton, Brent, Plymouth, Looe, Fowey, Tregony, Market Jew, Penzance, and St. Buryan. He tells of the formation of towns and shows natural features ; his maps also indicate the parish churches and the position of great houses and castles.

Other authorities opine that the Great Western Road enters Devonshire between the ninth and tenth milestones from Bridport, proceeding through Axminster and Kilmington to Honiton and from thence by Honiton Clyst and Heavitree to Exeter. From Exeter the road makes for Alphington to Chudleigh, and then on through Bickington to Ashburton, and so on to Buckfastleigh, South Brent, Ivybridge, and Plympton to Plymouth, its course through the county of Devon being approximately seventy-four miles.

Another road from Exeter to Plymouth branches off at Alphington and over Haldon to Newton Abbot, and so by Totnes to Ivybridge and Plymouth. Yet another road begins at Chudleigh and goes by Newton Abbot to Totnes and Ermington and so by the Laira Bridge to Plymouth. There is the road from Exeter to Starcross, Dawlish, and Teignmouth, as well as the direct road to the latter place, that passes over Haldon. From Newton Abbot there is the road to Torquay with branches to Paignton, Brixham, and Kingswear. Ashburton automatically becomes the centre for many places; it has a direct road to Totnes through Dartington; it has another to Tavistock, which meets the direct moorland road from Exeter to Tavistock at Two Bridges. The favourite and historical road from London to Falmouth and the Land's End leaves Exeter via Crockernwell and makes for Okehampton through South Zeal. The direct road from Exeter to Tavistock and Truro runs across the heights of Dartmoor by Two Bridges. Tavistock is brought into relationship with Devonport by a trunk road, and from Devonport to Saltash Ferry there is also a direct road. Tavistock is also on the trunk road from Plymouth to Launceston. Plymouth is connected to North Devon through Tavistock and Okehampton and from thence through Hatherleigh to Torrington, with branches to Bideford, Barnstaple, and Ilfracombe. From Exeter to Topsham a section of the old Great Western Road is encountered with branches to Otterton and Sidmouth and so to Salcombe Regis, Colyford, and Lyme Regis. The shorter road from Exeter to Sidmouth runs through Heavitree, Mary Clyst, and Newton Poppleford. In addition there is a direct road from Honiton through Sidbury to Sidmouth. The great road from Bath and Bristol runs through Bridgwater to Taunton and from thence through Cullompton to Bradninch, Broad Clyst, and Exeter. There are also other but more devious ways from Bath.

There is the coastal road from Bridgwater to Minehead which runs through Dunster to Dulverton, Bampton, and Tiverton, and a direct road from Tiverton to Barnstaple.

The road from Exeter to Barnstaple, about forty miles in length, passes through Crediton, Barrington, and Bishop's Tawton to Barnstaple. There is also a direct road from Crediton to Tiverton.

In Cornwall three main routes run westwards. The first is the direct artery from Okehampton to Launceston and Bodmin, which crosses Cardenham Moor by Car Green and Five Lanes and so by Truro and Redruth to Helston. There is the road from Launceston to Camelford and Padstow. The road from Tavistock to Callington, Liskeard, Lostwithiel, St. Austell, Grampound, and Truro, with tentacles to Penryn and Falmouth, and the lower roads through Saltash and Torpoint which take in St. Germans and Menheniot before entering Liskeard.

The western roads form a fascinating subject. Here the great actors from Elizabeth to Charles the Second, from Raleigh to Cromwell, William of Orange at Torbay, Monmouth at Sedgemoor and Judge Jeffreys at the Bloody Assize. Gay, too, may be visualised making his way to Exeter and immortalising the "Lamb" at Hartley Row. There are the architects, artists, and writers who in the past journeyed down to the west country too. Daniel Defoe, querulous and discursive; the famed Sir Christopher Wren; and later Sir John Vanbrugh, with his portfolio of plans to do the King's bidding at Plymouth Dock; James Gibbs, on his way to Antony House; Isaac Ware; the Paines; and Sir William Chambers as well as Robert Adam. There is the figure of James Wyatt on his way to Powderham Castle; of

Smeaton in his smart travelling chaise, built by Felton, with his schemes for the Eddystone and St. Ives. There is Joshua Reynolds, fresh from Plympton, setting out for London ; and at a later time Henry Holland going down to his estate near Okehampton. With Joseph Farington the roads can be traversed in good company, and the scenes he painted can be viewed as yet unsullied by industrial development. There is the energetic person of John Foulston hastening to Plymouth to weave his mantle of stucco about the three towns, as well as Daniel Alexander, the architect of Princetown, and the ubiquitous John Nash building " Stonelands " at Dawlish. From the early diary of Professor Cockerell can be gathered an impression of the western roads, the houses and the people. Again, one can turn to the time when Sir John Rennie had the Breakwater at Plymouth and the Victualling Yard in hand. The scene changes to the days of the railroad, with Brunel as chief magician, linking London to Bath, Bristol, and Exeter and performing his conjuring trick at Saltash. Still the figures come and go. There is Professor Donaldson going down to Exeter by the new railroad with his plans for the Italian villa at Shobrooke, while Wightwick operates at Plymouth and the neighbouring towns. The closer the subject is placed under the magnifying-glass the more apparent becomes the patterning of the tapestry to which those connected with the western region have added a contribution.

The coaching era reached its zenith when George the Fourth was king, and, as was fitting, the Devonport Mail gained the palm for sustained speed. For example, the Quicksilver Coach accomplished the 174 miles to Exeter in eighteen hours and on the up journey was scheduled over the same ground in seventeen hours, a performance truly wonderful. The coming of the railway speeded up matters, but old building traditions persisted, especially in Cornwall, and at a time when sequential design was practically abandoned in other parts of England, the craftsmen and builders of Devon and Cornwall sought no other inspiration than that to which they had become accustomed through years of experiment.

While upon the subject of railway development in Devon and Cornwall, the character of some of the buildings, which in the 'forties and 'fifties of the last century instanced the enterprise of *Railway Practice*, should be noticed. In the opening chapter the reader was led to Hyde Park Corner as a starting-point. The Victorians, with few exceptions, who preferred making the journey by private travelling carriage and looked askance at Brunel, took cab to Paddington and became part of Frith's picture. From London to Bristol many interesting railway buildings, now almost antique, will be seen. There is, for example, the older portion of the station at Reading, with its square turret and original clock ; there is the architectural framing of the Box tunnel, and the masonry and iron bridges forming the approach to Bath. The train shed at Exeter has lost its Victorian glass shade and thereby some part of the distinction it once shared with the " Lord of the Isles " and other big wheelers, but the Italianate tower is still in position, a relic of the " atmospheric line " to Plymouth. On the other hand, the wooden station and the stone-built sheds at Newton Abbot are genuine survivals. From Newton Abbot to Plymouth traces of the old railroad can be seen. At Ivybridge there is a representative station, and the wooden walls of North Road are as pleasant as is the reverse when the iron coruscations of Millbay Station meet the eye. Beyond Plymouth the changes have been fewer. There are the excellent Brunellesque designs of St. Germans, Menheniot, Liskeard, Doublebois, Lostwithiel, with their projecting canopies, spread out in rain and shine, like flat umbrellas. Here is direct evidence of environment on structure, the designer met the new conditions of travel in a reasonable manner and his works have stood the test of sixty years.

After the Napoleonic wars the western region, despite the decline of certain of its industries, entered upon another phase of its history. The period of the Regency witnessed the development of the seaside watering-places, such as Sidmouth, Exmouth, Dawlish, Teignmouth, and Torquay, all of which in their expansion attracted the attention of architects and builders. It was at this day that retired officers began to build the small villas which grace the slopes above Teignmouth and to occupy the terrace houses and villas of Plymouth, Stoke Damerel, and Torquay. The mining interest of Cornwall assumed a newer and fuller importance, due to the development of steam power and the installation of machinery on an extensive scale, while the shipyard at Plymouth, under the auspices of the Government, became the most important Naval centre in the country. It was due to improvements in machinery as well as to other inventions favoured by Sir Robert Seppings and Richard Pering in the construction of ships of the line that the building of warships at this period was concentrated at Devonport a hundred and twenty years after the formation of the Arsenal by William the Third. To the development of the Dockyard has been added the building of military and naval barracks, hospitals and administration buildings, all of which, especially in character, are closely allied with regional distinctions.

It will be apparent from a perusal of the foregoing chapters, as well as by investigation of the varied subjects selected as typical examples for illustration, that Devon and Cornwall conjointly have a traditional style peculiarly and wholly in harmony with the Dorian attitude of the west country. No other explanation, however investigations are conducted, could state the reasons for the surface differences which in the main are the outcome of the influence of material on structure. The fascination of the theme inheres in the straightforward acceptance by local builders, who in many instances acted as architects of the broad impulses and qualities of the major classic tradition which through the seventeenth, eighteenth and early nineteenth centuries became standard in Great Britain.

From the time of the Restoration until the year of the Great Exhibition the architecture of Devon and Cornwall reflected the interests of all classes in a manner quite distinct from the outlook in other parts. It is true that all materials were employed in the process, including brick, timber, and tiling; but in the main the material used was purely local, and if in working this material did not prove so susceptible to fine handling as did the materials available in other counties, it of necessity aided in the broadening of the accepted idea of well building. In the west country, in so far as building is concerned, it is the plain work that is of the greatest value, for it is free from the vulgarities of overcrowding, it has limitations imposed on license, and as architecture it is at once direct and convincing. Notwithstanding the apparent sameness of style, which at first sight seems inseparable from the average small house and cottage of the later periods in Devon and Cornwall, the differences of scale and finishing are innumerable. Every house is in reality different from its neighbour, except those arranged in terrace formations. As in Scotland and Ireland, the older houses have been built to meet particular requirements, and frequently depend for effect on the pleasant lines of the simple silhouette which is always in harmony with the natural setting. The chief attribute is that of human scale given by the doors and windows, the projection of the eaves, and the homely proportions of the whole. It is in detail an individual style, one cognisant of the composition of parts and one giving free scope to the idioms and whimsicalities of craftsmen. In the second half of the last century came the scourge of the builders' catalogue which swept regional tradition into the limbo of things unwanted. Then were built the motley villas of Plymouth, Truro, and Penzance ; then the hideous roofs of Newquay disgraced the older quarters of the town ; even Exeter forgot her ancestry and threw out the streets which are so depressing to eyes accustomed to conventional beauty. From this state of comparative confusion and mischance better things are slowly coming into force. In place of replicas of metropolitan villas of brick and Welsh slate with nondescript ornaments and cast-iron railings of bad design some architects are changing taste towards the reuse of local material. There is also a distinct movement towards a study of the abstract qualities of proportion and direct statement which form the chief attributes of old work. The desire for improvement is everywhere apparent, it does not lie in the direction of copying old work, neither does it propose to reproduce old forms which have served their day and purpose. On the contrary, it is modern in its application and has at heart the uplifting of building in general from the slough into which it has fallen during the past half-century.

To the town-planning movement of the last decade has succeeded the wider issue of regional development, which has as its aim and prerogative the preservation of local amenities. Both western counties at this present possess amenities unspoiled by exploitation, and it is the bounden duty of artists and authorities to take up the question of preservation with all the power at their command. In the past regional development arose at the call of local conditions, it resulted from a variety of interests and evolved its own methods of communication. The concentration of commercial interests in cities and towns intensified the need for ordered development which in other days was met by local enterprise and checked, to some extent, from becoming haphazard by the general feeling of good taste which then pertained. It was at this juncture a natural concomitant of town and country life, and did not assume unwieldy proportions until the second half of the nineteenth century.

To those engaged in forming the conventional scenery of Devon and Cornwall the thought rarely occurred, if at all, that the picture they were engaged upon was anything out of the common ; the buildings expressed distinctions of social status and occupation, there were definite rulings for farm-houses, cottages, and mansions, and an innate sense of right regarding the placing of buildings. In the growth of the villages and small towns is to be seen the persistence of mediæval custom, the necessity for protection as well as the persistence of the clannish and communal idea. There is, for example, the great house standing like a trusted chieftain with the dependents grouped significantly about. In the older parts of Exeter and

Plymouth can be seen the mediæval shapings of timber and stone which during Georgian days were decked out with new costumes to suit changing fashions, and in this regard it is astonishing how much of Tudor England still exists. The mediæval tendencies, not only in the working of material, but more particularly in the grouping of houses on hilly sites, resulted in picturesque formations. The old fishing villages of Devon and Cornwall are pregnant with vistas of narrow streets and alleys, where the houses jostle in the most friendly and neighbourlike way. As the eighteenth century progressed so the western towns, from introducing isolated houses of formal character on open sites adjacent to old quarters, began to consider, through the good offices of local surveyors, the need for formal development. There are the example of the Exeter crescents and the straight-fronted terraces; the crescents and squares of Plymouth as well as the lesser streets of Stonehouse, Devonport, Truro, and Penzance. The mining villages of Cornwall present another aspect of the picture. Those which came into being at the beginning of the nineteenth century, such as the villages of Cheesewring, Gunnislake, and the outer streets of Bodmin and Truro, in part inherit the tendencies of mediæval grouping and stepping combined with the decorum of worked masonry and neatly sashed windows. When

THE CUSTOMS HOUSE, HAYLE. 1812.

Alexander designed the houses in the main street at Princetown he had recourse to the stepped method of grouping, and was enabled by such means to combine small houses of different size into a harmonious grouping.

There is no mistaking the homely charm of the small houses of the west country, which make a direct appeal by reason of their simplicity. It is towards such exemplars that attention is especially directed; it is a consistent style and one which asserts the principle of proper standardisation. It is common to the whole of Cornwall and is seen in miniature at St. Mary's in the Isles of Scilly. There are the especial factors of detail which every architect should note, such as the retention of a marginal frame within a recessed reveal for the windows, the judicious use of local slate in diminishing course for the roofs, the right detail for chimney cappings, the use of slate for sills and floors as well as for weatherings and offsets. There are considerations of weatherproofing and the need for storm-porches. Regarding planning, time-honoured customs of living should be observed. There is, for example, the Cornish custom of placing the table in the living room near the window, and on occasion giving preference to the fireside being on the front of the house and near a window, as at Polperro and St. Ives. With the development of education the people of the west country are prone to look down on the simple faring of their ancestors and to scorn the lovable qualities of the old homes and their inconveniences. All the foregoing can be granted, but it is not an excuse for indiscriminate haste in exchanging old lamps for new and forsaking the substance for the shadow. The regional style, as evidenced in the homes of the people, is just as worthy of study as the polite artificialities of the great houses, it is the building expression of a people

N

THE MARKET HOUSE, PENZANCE. 1836.
William Harris, of Bristol, Architect.

proud of their freedom and independence, it is democratic in a fine way and if lacking in finesse makes up for this deficiency by honesty of purpose.

At this present, when so much is being undertaken in the interests of the community to improve housing conditions and to bring into force the great blessings of health and cleanliness, attention to the artistic sense of propriety is equally essential. As far as domestic building is concerned vast improvements have been effected in planning, but, sad to relate, these have not been accompanied by good taste in the outward aspect. The new conditions do not require portentous handling or even the palest reflection of mock gentility. There is no room for architect's architecture or that worst form of snobbishness, the speculative builder's caricature of the work of architects. The existing prejudice of the people against simplicity of statement in house building must be overcome, not by local legislation or Act of Parliament, but by a gradual realisation among the people themselves of the value of the historical evidences amidst which they live and work. It costs no more to build plainly and with taste than it does to bedizen a small house with catalogue ornaments.

It is the purpose of this book to focus attention on the buildings of Devon and Cornwall, apart from the churches, and to lay particular stress on the inherent charm of the later domestic work. It will be seen from the exemplars that the regional development resulted from the gradual fusion of ideas gathered from various sources. The nature of the country and its natural materials determined the main issues, while experience of taste and fashion in other parts of England served to vitalise dormant tendencies and to bring the same to a standard which was at once consistent and logical. It will be observed that commerce and local industry were important concomitants, and that the spirit of the west country through such agencies has been crystallised from the abstract into the concrete. What is true of the west country applies equally to the other regional districts of England ; but Devon and Cornwall are unique in traditional values which have outlived time.

INDEX

INDEX TO ILLUSTRATIONS